Someone Else's Child

Olive Stevenson
Professor of Social Policy and Social Work
University of Keele

Revised Edition

Rout
Lond

First published in 1965
This revised edition published in 1977
by Routledge & Kegan Paul Ltd,
39 Store Street,
London WC1E 7DD,
Broadway House,
Newtown Road,
Henley-on-Thames,
Oxon RG9 1EN and
9 Park Street,
Boston, Mass. 02108, USA
Photoset in 11 on 12pt Baskerville
by Kelly and Wright, Bradford-on-Avon, Wiltshire
and printed in Great Britain by
Page Bros Ltd, Norwich

British Library Cataloguing in Publication Data

Stevenson, Olive

Someone else's child—Revised ed.
1. Foster home care—Great Britain
I. Title
362.7'33'0941   HV887.G5   77–30109

ISBN 0 7100 8706 3

Contents

Preface

This revised version of *Someone Else's Child*, first published in 1965, comes at a time when the role of foster parents has been receiving renewed attention and there have been some significant legal changes, embodied in the Children Act 1975. I have tried to take account of the shifts in emphasis both in relation to the kinds of children available for fostering and the foster parents' rights and responsibilities. But recent much publicised cases have tended to blur a crucially important fact — that many thousands of young children require loving, sensitive *short-term* care when their parents are in difficulties. The service such foster parents perform is no more, and no less, valuable than that provided by those who care for smaller numbers of children over longer periods. Thus, there was a need to keep a balance in the book to allow for the many variations on the fostering theme, all of which bring different problems and rewards.

In the interests of brevity, I will not here repeat my thanks to those who helped me so much, directly and indirectly, in shaping the book. Perhaps the fact that substantial sections did not seem to me to need revision is an indication of their lasting influence. More recently, however, my thanks are due to Jane Aldgate, Kenneth Brill and Brian McGinnis for advice on various points.

1

Children away from home

Why this book was written

This book is primarily intended for the foster parents of younger children — that is children under five. It may be, however, that it will also be of some use to others: to foster parents of older children, because there is much in it that applies to fostering in general; to the staff of residential establishments or to nurses in hospitals, and to some 'daily minders'. Some of the topics discussed are fundamental to all children separated from their parents.

Although I have chosen to focus on young children, I fully recognise that, in many respects, the difficulties of fostering older children are even greater, since they often find it less easy to adapt to the ways of a different family and to make new relationships. However, one must begin somewhere: I have begun with the first five years because it is now generally agreed that the experiences of these first years are of great significance for the later development of the child, physically, mentally and emotionally.* Therefore when a young child leaves his parents everyone involved carries a heavy responsibility. In this book I am going to discuss many different ways in which I believe greater understanding and knowledge will help foster parents to help children more. This is not just

* There is abundant evidence for this from many different kinds of studies in all parts of the world. Foster parents will be especially interested in Bowlby's *Child Care and the Growth of Love* (Penguin, 1970) but this only deals with one of the many aspects of the subject.

because we want to be kind to children, but because of the crucial importance of their early years.

There are especially good reasons why foster parents need to know more about the behaviour of children and adults — including themselves. There was a time when many foster parents took a child into their homes hoping to make him one of their own, hoping for something which was like adoption. They wanted the same kind of satisfactions that ordinary parents get from bringing up their own children — and sometimes it worked out like that. For such people, you could say the 'joys of parenthood' were enough; they did not need any other satisfaction. But times have changed. Fewer children are available as babies for adoption. Greater use of birth control and the changed social climate which makes it possible for some unmarried mothers to keep their babies with them, have reduced the numbers of 'straight-forward' babies for couples to adopt.

Fact, figures and reasons

Those who foster, therefore, will very rarely find themselves in a situation like that of adoptive parents of a previous generation. They are needed in the main for five groups of young children.

(1) By far the largest group of children who come into care of local authorities do so for short periods because of the illness of the mother, or the birth of a new baby. In 1972, for example, in England alone, there were about 20,000 such children. It can be assumed that most of these were under five, most will have gone home before long and that many will have been fostered.

(2) There is a small, but not insignificant, number of children in care of local authorities who are physically or

mentally handicapped and who will benefit from the care of an ordinary family life. Some of these children would have died in earlier years. Medical advance has brought its own problems. They live on and have the right to as normal and permanent a home life as can be provided.

(3) A small number of children are removed from home because their parents have neglected or ill-treated them. They are likely to be fostered for a long time, if not permanently, and will probably be the subject of 'care orders', which gives the local authority parental powers.

(4) A group which pose special difficulties for foster parents are children who come into care 'temporarily' and voluntarily because of their parents' difficulties, such as mental illness or homelessness, but for whom the length of stay cannot be predicted.

(5) A large number of young children are not in local authority care but are fostered privately by their parents. Such foster parents are obliged to register with the local authority and it has been estimated that there may be about 12,000 such children, of whom the overwhelming proportion are under five. It is reasonable to assume that there are probably several thousand more not registered because their foster parents are unaware of the regulations or unwilling to conform with them. The reasons for such arrangements are many and various but in some parts of the country research has shown that a very high proportion of these privately fostered children had West African parents who were students. This was found by Robert Holman whose book *Trading in Children* (Routledge & Kegan Paul, 1973) is not unsympathetic to private foster parents, as the title might suggest.

There are some young children fostered who are in the care of voluntary organisations, such as Dr Barnado's and the Church of England Children's Society; however, such organisations have been of late re-thinking their role and have been experimenting with special community provision rather than offering a service parallel to that of local authorities. There are also many children away from home for long or short periods in residential nurseries and in hospitals — physical and mental.

In short, every year probably about half a million young children leave their parents for a time and of these at least half are fostered. In addition, there are very large numbers of children 'daily minded' both in private families and in various forms of crèche.

We know that even a day with strangers or even with familiar relatives is an adventure to a young child and not a completely care-free one. It is usually a mixture of doubts and fears as well as pleasure and excitement. What happens to children in the first years of life and how these happenings are managed is undoubtedly of great significance to their future development. These figures show us that a large number of adults will be concerned in one way or another with many thousands of children away from home. The adults deserve help, for it is a service which must not be undertaken lightly. It is to these 'care-givers' that this book is addressed.

One difficult, thorny matter arising from this cannot be passed over. If we speak of foster parents as doing a 'highly skilled job', it is natural for the question to be asked: 'What about payment?'

The position at present is that the majority of foster parents are paid only enough to cover the cost of taking a child into their family — and many foster parents say that the sums paid do not even cover this. Some local authorities pay special rates to foster parents who take on children with special problems, for example, handi-capped children, but it is generally true to say that the idea of 'making a profit' or—in fact—earning money from fostering has not been widely accepted.

Some people may feel that this is meanness on the part of the local authority committees and there is no doubt we cannot leave this out of account: it is pointed out how much more it costs to keep a child in residential care. We must, however, recognise that there is another reason for not paying foster parents more—the fear that people might 'do it for the money', not for love of the child. It can also be argued that if people are bringing up a child as one of their own—with all the pleasure that this implies—this could be reward enough; however, there are fewer of such 'near adoptions' as the years go by, for the reasons I have discussed above.

If foster parents are increasingly asked to play a role which is different from that of an ordinary parent, the question of payment 'for a job' is bound to arise. My own view is that there is nothing incompatible between loving and caring for the child and making some money. After all, staff of children's homes get salaries and nobody suggests now that they care for children less well because of it. But all good foster parents will realise that where the life and happiness of a child is at stake, it is very important to choose people whose primary motive is one of concern for children and their families. For there were in the past many appalling cases of children taken 'for profit' and grossly neglected, and the memories of these cases linger on. In my opinion, the ultimate safeguard is not to keep payments low but to choose foster parents with great care and skill; but the latter is a difficult task.

None the less, many of us feel that the time has now come when social workers and foster parents should work together for a realistic payment to people who choose to look after children rather than pursue a career outside the home. More and more women are going out to work; planned families ensure that they are not tied as in the past. Society cannot any longer take advantage of the 'captive housewife'. As this book will show, the emotional demands of fostering are considerable and the level of skill needed high. The financial rewards should take account of this, not least to accord foster parents in the wider society a richly deserved status as 'skilled workers'.

Foster parents of young children who are handicapped will find a situation in relation to special allowances which is rather unsatisfactory. Some local authorities do, of course, pay special allowances for the care of such children but these vary across the country. There has been considerable controversy, and questions asked in the House of Commons, about the payment of an attendance allowance to foster parents caring for a severely handicapped child. So far, foster parents are not entitled to this allowance as are parents of similarly handicapped children over two years old. (An attendance allowance is payable at two rates, currently £8.15 and £12.20 weekly if a doctor certifies that the person needs 'constant attendance' by day *or* by day *and* night.)

Of course, were such allowances payable to foster parents by central government, local authorities might deduct such sums from their allowances. It may be that foster parents lose out as the battle between central and local government continues!

Another benefit, known as mobility allowance (currently £5 weekly), is available to some severely handicapped persons over the age of five. Some, of whom I am one, think the age should be lowered, at least to age two, by which time a normal child is fully mobile. Foster parents may wish to 'join forces' with parents in pressing for this.

Of course, there are other benefits not connected with handicap, of which the newest is Child Benefit. Once again, the situation is complicated and you should get it straight in your case either with your social worker or social security.

What all this adds up to is a muddle. Some of us think it is high time it was cleared up. In the meanwhile, it is safest for me to say — ask about your particular case, rather than raising false hopes.

Social service departments and their social workers

Those who fostered for the local authority before 1970 will have known the 'children's departments', with the 'children's officer' and the 'child care officers' who worked in them. In 1970,* various different parts of the welfare services, which had been in separate departments were brought together under one umbrella, the social service departments. This meant that pesonal services to everyone in need, for instance, the elderly, the physically or mentally handicapped, families in trouble, as well as those for children in care, were the responsibility of one department in the local authority. In many parts of England, Wales and Scotland, there followed soon afterwards another reorganisation of local government areas. This meant that some social service departments found themselves 'under new management', as it were. It is important for foster parents to realise that those who visit them (and those who pay them!) may have undergone two upheavals in the last few years.

---

* Scots readers will know that these changes took place earlier in 1968, and the equivalent department was called the 'social work department'. Northern Ireland foster parents have as their equivalent the 'health and social service boards', created in 1974.

It is early days to assess the long-term advantages and disadvantages of such major changes but I expect that there are some foster parents who feel they have had a less satisfactory service from the new style departments than they had from the old 'children's departments'. It may be helpful to explain some of the reasons why this may have happened.

(1) Large scale organisational change affects everybody. More people changed their jobs to fit the new patterns and many practical matters have had to be worked out. For instance, different people may have taken over foster parents' payments, perhaps as part of other financial responsibilities. Muddles may result!

(2) Groups of social workers came together, usually in 'area teams', who had previously worked in different departments and had often had different kinds of training. It has taken time to shake down together and to decide who does what. There has been much argument about this and it is still going on. Some foster parents will know of the debate about 'generic' and 'specialist' social workers. It would take too long to go into all the pros and cons in this book but I can perhaps clear the ground a little.

There was nothing in the reorganisation itself which made it impossible for individual social workers to specialise in work with people in whose needs they were especially interested. In fact, in many areas, informal kinds of specialisation are developing. However, it is not as obvious as may seem at first sight that social workers should, or need to, choose on the basis of the old categories. For instance, a social worker might be interested in finding substitute homes, foster homes or lodgings, for a range of people, children, the mentally handicapped and even the elderly. Foster parents of young children might find that they shared many common interests and problems with others who cared for adults in need of a home life and a social worker might specialise in the understanding of these interests and problems. What is happening at present is very confusing to social workers because there is no clear trend developing. Small wonder if foster parents feel confused too! One thing, however, is clearly and urgently needed. As some of the older social workers move to senior jobs or retire, some of the special knowledge of children in care which they had is no longer readily available to new staff, whether trained or untrained. It is absolutely essential, therefore, that special training should be given to a certain number of staff to support the ordinary social worker and perhaps to carry especially difficult cases, as for example when relationships between parents and foster parents are very complicated. Otherwise foster parents will not get the kind of support they need and deserve.

Meanwhile, it may fall sometimes to the experienced foster mother to remind the social worker of some of the matters crucially important to this child when he is received into care. (I discuss these in chapter 3.) It may do no harm if foster parents show this to the social workers if they are not happy at the way the reception is being handled!

(3). It would be quite unfair to attribute all the present troubles of social service departments to reorganisation of one kind or another. There are at least five other major reasons.

First, at about the same time as reorganisation, social services had new and time-consuming duties placed upon them in relation to children in trouble and disabled people. It is generally agreed they were not adequately staffed to meet those demands.*

Second, inflation and unemployment have caused many families on low incomes or social security to fall into debt in certain major items such as rent, fuel, etc., and social service departments have been increasingly asked to 'plug the gaps'. This takes up much social work time.

Third, there has been, as all foster parents will know, a wave of public anxiety about physical ill-treatment of children by their parents. I shall return to this later. For the moment, I simply point out that this anxiety has resulted in a greater proportion of social workers' time being spent on such problems — not only visiting the families but attending case conferences and so on.

Fourth, despite a huge expansion of training in the 1960s, only about half the field workers in social service departments are fully qualified. This is because the numbers required continued to expand as fast as training places increased.

Fifth, shortages of trained staff have meant that in many parts of the country staff have not stayed in their jobs as long as one would wish. There are a number of reasons for this, sometimes promotions, sometimes a move to get training, sometimes, sadly, leaving social work from sheer exhaustion.

Before 1970, there were great variations in the quality of the child care service in the local authority. It does not do to idealise the past. Some foster parents will have unhappy memories of their contact with the old children's departments. Nevertheless, others will probably feel that the old departments offered them a more direct personal service, perhaps with greater continuity of

* The two Acts conferring these duties were the Children and Young Persons Act 1969 and the Chronic Sick and Disabled Persons Act 1970. Similar provisions exist in Scotland though not in Northern Ireland.

staff. We cannot turn the clock back, nor should I, for one, wish to do so. What the new social service departments will have to create, however, is some new kind of caring structure so that foster parents know they can depend on a reliable team of social workers who have readily available specialist advice and who are sensitive to the needs of all the people involved in situations which can be emotionally complicated even in so-called 'straightforward' short-stay placements. It may be that foster parents will now begin to organise themselves locally to bring pressure to bear on departments if they do not feel well enough supported.

In this aspect of their work, social workers have a number of tasks. They must investigate applications for reception into care and, if necessary, make the arrangements, although their first duty is to see if alternative plans can be made to avoid reception. (Where neglect or ill-treatment is suspected, they may have to remove a child with an order from the magistrate. In that case, the child is usually brought later to a juvenile court and may be removed from home on a 'care order'.) Whatever the circumstances, however, it is the social worker who must plan the substitute care for the child who is away from home.

Social workers, not necessarily the same ones, must also investigate applications to foster. The home must be visited, references taken up and so on.

If a child in care is placed in a foster home a social worker has a legal duty to visit at regular intervals to make sure the child is well cared for, physically and emotionally.

If there is parental contact, the social worker should be involved in this and, where appropriate, work with everyone towards the child's return to his natural parents.

If a child is privately fostered, the social worker has a responsibility to ensure his welfare but his powers and duties are much less clearly defined. It is not, for example, laid down how often he should visit the foster home as it is for children in care.

These are the bare bones. Anyone who has fostered knows that every one of these tasks can be complicated and can be handled well or badly. Some of the feelings they arouse will be discussed later, as well as the legal position of different children in care and the implications for foster parents. For the moment, I simply describe that part of the social worker's job with which the foster parent comes into contact.

The description highlights one inescapable fact: that the social worker has a mixture of roles in relation to foster parents and the mixture is sometimes uncomfortable for one or both parties. However sure you personally are that the care you give your foster child is good and loving, you will acknowledge the need for such children to be protected. For it is a sad fact that children have been, and sometimes still are, neglected or ill-treated in their foster homes.

Local authority 'children's departments' were set up in 1948 partly as a result of the neglect or death of a foster child.* Recent cases, widely reported in the media, have tended to emphasise ill-treatment by parents. But foster parents are also on occasion a prey to the same angry emotions and there have been some recent cases which illustrate this, less widely reported. It is, therefore, quite inevitable that the social worker, backed by statutory regulations, is in one sense an inspector. It is far better if

* The Dennis O'Neill case, when the death of a little boy in his foster home started enquiries which led to far-reaching changes in the organisation of care for deprived children.

this is faced openly between social workers and foster parents because, although it is important, it is only one aspect of the relationship. The more candour there can be the better.

If all is well, visiting foster homes can be one of the most cheering and rewarding aspects of the social worker's day. Indeed, I can remember hoping I would not hear anything was wrong, which I fear made it very likely I did not pick up the hints foster parents may have dropped! But there is nothing more agreeable than seeing a child flourish in a good foster home. However, in many successful fosterings, the foster parents need, at some time or another, some kind of support, practical or emotional. It may be to do with the child or with his parents. They have a right to expect it to be forthcoming for they do a demanding and, at times, exhausting job for the community. The relationships with social workers should be one in which they can look for that support and, on occasions, advice. Even if foster parents know as much or more about bringing up children as do the social workers, they may not know their way round the social services, and they may need someone who will listen with sensitive understanding to the accumulated frustrations which difficult children and parents can cause.

I write this in the full knowledge that at present foster parents do not always get this support. But, ten years after writing the first edition of this book, I remain convinced that this is the kind of relationship which they should hope to establish with each other. That this work is accepted as essential to good social work practice is reflected in the recent government publication *Foster Care* (HMSO, 1976) which sets out in much detail the responsibilities of social workers in their relationships with all involved in fostering.

14 Children away from home

Some useful books

J. Heywood, *Children in Care*, Routledge & Kegan Paul, 1959.
J. Packman, *The Child's Generation*, Blackwell, 1975.
(Two 'solid' books about the history of the child care service.)
R. Holman, 'The Place of Fostering in Social Work',
  British Journal of Social Work, 1975, vol. 5, no. 1.
(For anyone interested in what we know now of success and
failure in fostering.)
T. Parker, *Five Women*, Hutchinson, 1965.
J. Hitchman, *King of the Barbareens*, Penguin, 1971.
N. Timms, *The Receiving End*, Routledge & Kegan Paul,
  1973.
F. Norman, *Banana Boy*, Secker & Warburg, 1969.
(Personal accounts by former children in care or people in
trouble.)
R. Evans, *Happy Families?*, Peter Owen, 1977.
(A biography by a social worker in child care.)

2 Ordinary children

Foster children are not 'ordinary' because they have had to come away from home; they are not ordinary because sometimes they may be unusually difficult or unhappy. But they *are* ordinary in the sense that they are trying to develop in the same way as any other child. So we must therefore first consider the development of ordinary children.

However, this is in no sense a comprehensive study of the topic; there are useful books already available which do this excellently.* I want to pick out certain aspects which seem to me particularly important. There are two questions which can usefully be asked. What is the ordinary young child trying to achieve and how does he achieve it? He is trying to grow up; that is obvious enough. But what is really involved in growing up? He has only made a start by the time he is five; indeed the things I am going to describe go on, in a way, throughout life and do not end at five, fifteen or twenty-five. But the start that is made in the first five years is of very great importance for his future happiness.

There are three struggles going on in the young child — all connected with one another, yet distinct — each a part of growing up:

(1) There is the struggle between loving oneself and loving other people.

(2) There is the struggle between wanting to belong

* See the list at the end of this chapter.

and wanting to be separate.

(3) There is the struggle between the 'real' world, as the grown ups see it, and the imaginary world of the child.

Self-love and other love

A baby is a completely self-centred little object; he is the prime example of 'Blow you, I'm all right Jack'. No one minds about this—it is 'normal'. So long as he is comfortable, nothing else matters to him! Comfortable does not mean just having food inside him and clean clothes—if that were so babies in the past in institutions who were well looked after physically, but not loved, would have been comfortable—and they were not. They were sad, miserable and listless. Comfortable for a baby includes being close to his mother, in a kind of world of their own, almost as close as before he was born. He is not interested in how his mother is feeling, except in so far as it affects him and he is very angry when he is hungry or has a pain. All that is obvious. But by what marvellous process does that baby turn into a loving, patient, concerned father—waiting for his tea till his baby has been fed, and getting up in the middle of a heavy sleep to attend to his squalling infant? Even more remarkable, how does that baby grow into a man capable of being concerned about many other people, relations, work-mates and so on—not just his own children, which you might just put down to 'paternal instinct' and leave it at that? Gradually, almost imperceptibly, the baby and the child begin to understand a bit about other people's needs and feelings and to mind about them. The story of the first five years is the story of an enormous achievement, for here we see concern for other people — in the first instance usually the parents — beginning to be an active force in the child's behaviour. We know that good solid foundations for 'other-love' are laid in these first years and that although human beings may learn to love others later on, they have a hard job of it if they did not begin well then.

How does it begin? Those of you who have had children will know that in the early weeks and months of life a baby is not really aware of a whole person. He is aware obviously of all kinds of sensations, for instance of his mother's breast or of being tightly held, but it does not seem likely that he thinks to himself — 'ah, that is my mother or my father'. A baby's smiles begin early but there develops later a very special smile which every mother recognises as a signal that he has recognised her particularly — it is not just a response to any adult standing above him. At that moment, you become a person to him as he has been a person to you since he was born. I wonder when you think this happens. Some people think at about six months. Clearly, whenever it happens, it is the beginning of other-love. People are no longer just objects — useful extensions of the baby's world bringing him food and comfort. That makes a difference to everything. The baby somehow realises that the person towards whom he feels loving when he is fed is the same person towards whom he feels angry when he is hungry. Is this where the ability to feel sorry and guilty for our bad feelings begins? How early have you noticed this in children? Some experts believe that it begins right back in the first year of life after this recognition by the baby of a whole person different from any other takes place. It does not matter too much to ordinary parents when this actually begins — the main thing is that the child, having recognised 'whole people', is learning to accept the fact that love can go on working even though he is angry and cross with the loved ones and that love comes out on top in the end.

When all this actually begins may matter more to foster parents for various reasons, but that will be discussed in the next chapter. Ordinary parents can see the beginnings of the real two-way relationship in lots of ways; they can see it when they feed their ten-month baby and he tries to put the spoon to their mouth. He is pleased if they pretend to eat what he gives them, but he is not yet anywhere near actually *giving* them his share—that is many years hence. He is trying out the idea of giving to see what it feels like and he would be surprised and probably upset if they actually ate it. It can be seen when, with the birth of a new baby, the two-year-old struggles with his jealousy and manages, with help, to hold the baby gently in his arms on the settee. Never mind that a few minutes later, he pokes her in the eye. The battle between love and jealousy is raging inside him but the ordinary child wins the battle, or babies all over the country would be damaged beyond repair. It can be seen a little later over the question of 'sharing the parents'. For gradual extensions of love from the close one-to-oneness of a mother and baby to include others, each of whom has his own ties to the others, is the first great lesson of sharing that has to be learnt. Loving others includes letting other people love each other. Every ordinary parent has examples of the times when his three- or four-year-old invents 'when I'm grown up' stories which include one parent and exclude the other from the set up, but in the end he settles down to not having all the shares in the company.

Perhaps the way in which the beginnings of other-love show most clearly are in the efforts the child makes to conform to the behaviour expected of him. There are other reasons for this as well. One reason is the child's wish to be like the grown-ups — and the urge to imitate is very strong. Another reason is fear of the consequences of misbehaviour. *Some* fear is inevitable and necessary and not unhelpful because the young child has not got sufficient control *inside* himself yet and so the knowledge that he will get a smack for jumping on the flower beds is quite useful. Too much fear is of course bad because it does not help the important lasting control to develop. Instead of: 'I will not do this because it upsets my mother and I love my mother and I do not wish to upset her' we are left with: 'I will not do this because I will get beaten; but I would do it if I were sure I would not be found out.' Now some of this last reasoning stays with us always from childhood onwards and fear of the consequences always plays a part in making us behave ourselves. But it is clear that in a healthy child there is also developing the self-control which springs from loving feelings for other people. In the child under five we see the intense effort which is put into it. Take the matter of toilet training. He is not naturally clean and dry; he feels no disgust about the products of his own body — quite the contrary he is very interested in them and will play with his motions when his nappy comes off. Yet within two or three years, he has learnt — more or less — to do what the grown-ups want. This is not simply 'habit training' as some people used to think. We know it is not from experiences with children who had been in residential nurseries. When children were 'trained clean' rather than 'loved clean', it was found that however obedient they might be while in the nursery, the cleanliness broke down when they were moved or fostered and the process had to start all over again from scratch. I am not just speaking of a few wet beds or dirty pants—I mean a total breakdown of the toilet training which often took years to right itself. The ordinary child gets clean partly because he learns this is a way to please his parents, a way to show his love for them and be loved in return.

You will notice that I have not written about 'unselfishness'. I have been writing about the child's growth of love for others but this does not mean learning *not* to love himself. For in a complicated way, the one feeds into the other. In the early months and years of life, the ordinary child—quite unconsciously—is learning a vital truth. First he is loved; this starts him off loving back; thus he gets more love in return and so on. This is the birthright of the ordinary child and the tragedy of some deprived children is that the opposite has happened; he was not loved first of all; so he could not learn how to love back; so he was not loved in return and so on in a series of dismal failures in relationship all through childhood. Proper self-love begins through being loved and valued; as a mother holds and feeds her baby, she conveys to him that he is uniquely valuable to her and she shows this in dozens of ways through his childhood. So this certainty of being loved brings a deep sense of one's own value and worth which is utterly different from being 'conceited' or 'cocky'. In the first year of life the ordinary child learns he is lovable and he learns to love others. This is the first central achievement upon which so much else depends.

The struggle of wanting to belong and wanting to be separate

Think of the beginnings of life inside the womb; think of the twenty-year-old getting married and leaving the home; then think of the years between. It is clear that although the physical cord was cut at the baby's birth, there is a psychological cord which is uncut all through childhood and adolescence; some would say it is never really cut even in adult life or after the parents' death. As I said earlier, in the first few weeks of a baby's life, an ordinary mother and her baby make a kind of world of their own* which is like, but not quite like, the situation before he was born. Then slowly but surely, the baby is helped to realise that he is not just a part of his mother; he is separate. He discovers where he ends and other things begin; the boundaries of his body. He gradually gets a sense of 'one-ness', of identity. 'My name is Tommy and I live at 33, High Street, Brookford and I am three.' Yet on the other hand, there is a continuing need to be as close and as 'together' as possible. All our lives we try to reconcile these different kinds of need and to find a balance between them; people in love delight in a special feeling of 'togetherness'; even in death, the final separation, we have phrases like 'returning to mother earth' to comfort us with an idea of union again with a mother. Yet pulling against this is the desire to prove we can be independent, that we do not depend on one another for life itself, as the baby does in the womb. You can see this struggle very clearly in the first few years of life. For example, you can see it in the gradually increasing length of time the child can bear to be apart from his mother without anxiety; there is a considerable difference between a two- and a four-year-old in this respect — watch how many times in a morning they return to 'check up' on the grown-ups. It is as if that psychological cord was made of elastic with infinite

* Those interested in this idea might read the first chapters of D. W. Winnicott's *The Child, the Family and the Outside World*, Penguin, 1964.

stretch; month by month the child stretches it a bit further but every now and again something happens and then suddenly ping! it snaps back and he needs to be close and tight to her again.

In this, as in every aspect of child development, we cannot separate physical, emotional and mental aspects one from the other; for as the ordinary child grows physically and mentally more independent of his parents so his emotional independence is also increased.

The family is a splendid place for the child to begin to find a satisfactory balance between these two opposing needs. For the fact of being loved, as I have said, does give a child a feeling of being special and separate. 'I am me and nobody else.' The family acknowledges this in many ways. 'John likes cornflakes better than rice crispies.' 'Yellow is Mary's favourite colour'; 'Kevin likes the curtains drawn at night; Kathleen doesn't.' Yet on the other hand, the relationship, first with mother and later with the whole family, gives a sense of belonging and of closeness that nothing else can rival. So ordinary parents help their children to be separate and yet a part of something at one and the same time. One of the most important ways in which this is done is in the management of the young child's angry feelings and outbursts of rebellion. For these are healthy and necessary in the process of becoming separate. The young child must be able to challenge and disobey, and his parents have a perfect right to be angry and punish him if they feel like it. The harmful thing is when a child feels he dare not show his anger in case he hurts his mother, for this makes 'separating out' more difficult. On the other hand, the fact that he is held within his family and accepted despite all these outbursts gives him a certainty of belonging more profound than anything else.

The world outside and the world inside

One of the marvels of human life is the speed with which the young child learns about the world around him. The human baby takes longer to grow up than any other animal but what he learns in the process is complicated and extensive.

Consider this detailed description of how he learns about the telephone. There are hundreds of other similar discoveries about ordinary things in the first years of life — about the cooker, the boiler, the car, the garden, and so on.

The small child becomes aware of a sudden sound. The sound starts and stops. Sometimes it is so loud it wakes you up. After a while the child learns that the sound happens in the same corner of the room where there is a black (or today it may be a red or yellow or blue) thing that comes apart into two parts, a thing that mother or father sometimes holds. Then the child learns that when one part is picked up, still connected by a cord to the other part (but 'connected' is too hard an idea, still somehow part of the other part), the sound stops. This is a great discovery. Someone goes to the telephone, picks up one part of it; the sound of ringing stops. This is a piece of a pattern. It will happen again. Instead of being frightened when the telephone rings, the child can wait and watch; soon, someone will come and pick up the receiver, and the ringing will stop. The next discovery may come weeks or months later. A telephone is something to talk to. Mother or father picks up the receiver and talks into it. The child waits for that, too, and learns that after the talking, the receiver will be put back where it was when the ringing began. This, too, is a piece of a pattern, something understood and expected. The next step, more wonderfully exciting perhaps than the others, comes when the receiver is placed at the child's ear and he hears a voice, a familiar voice, Daddy's voice.

The child has accumulated information about telephones. Where the ring comes from, what makes the ringing stop, what grown-ups do when it rings, that if you listen you can hear someone talking when the someone isn't in the room. There is a telephone in Grandma's house, too, and you can hear Grandma's voice on your home telephone and mother's voice on Grandma's telephone. A child who lives in the country learns that those tall wooden poles are called telephone poles. The part of the telephone called the receiver is fastened to the other part by a long black string, the telephone is fastened to the wall by another long black string, and there are long strings between the telephone poles. The child asks, 'Can I telephone Daddy?' Mother explains, 'Not just now, because Daddy has left his office. He is on the way home.' On his way home, driving in the car, on the road where the telephone poles are, but. . . . A question, 'Is there a telephone in Daddy's car?' Again mother explains, 'No, Tommy, a telephone needs wires, you see.' What is a wire? Strings, cords, wires that hum, a telephone at Grandma's and at the office where Daddy works and here, but no telephone in Daddy's car . . . suddenly the whole complicated pattern takes shape. The telephones stay in places, the wires go between. 'Mummy, can I telephone Grandma?' This is the *creative* moment.*

---

* Margaret Mead, *A Creative Life for your Children*.

It is only by studying as closely as this the step-by-step detail of the discovery that we get any idea of how complicated it is, and when we multiply that experience by hundreds, we begin to understand how remarkable the ordinary young child is! The small baby's world is one of sensations, broken up and fleeting. He knows only how he feels. As I have suggested he learns gradually about other people, and himself in relation to them. But he also learns about the objects that make up his world; how they work, how they connect with each other and what use he can make of them. This begins with the world inside the pram or cot, then it becomes the world inside the room (and how exhausting this phase can be for the parents!) and from that it gradually widens further and further. Every healthy child is by nature an explorer and at every age there are things to protect him from and risks that have to be taken. It is obvious that all this must be gone through if the child is to grow to a normal adult, knowledgeable enough to 'find his way about', as we say. But there is another reason for helping the child find out about what we call 'the real world'; that is, to balance the power which his imaginary world has over him. Here is an extract from an actual piece of observation at a nursery school. There are three little boys playing together; Anthony is a large, bossy little boy; Paul and Simon are three, both in their different ways rather nervous children.

Anthony:	'Who wants to go into a magic rocket? It's rather high for you. You'll bump on the moon. Hang on there to me.'
Paul:	(goes to the teacher and takes her hand), saying: 'You be Mummy rocket and I'll be boy rocket.'

Anthony:	'I'll be the biggest rocket in the world.' (Dashing round.)
Paul:	'Not *really*.'
Anthony:	'We'll make it. We know what to do, don't we, Paul?'
Paul:	(with increasing nervousness): 'We're going to be rockets.'
Anthony:	'Boys first, not grown ups.'
Simon:	(has been watching, goes red and sucks his thumb): 'Not want to.'
Paul:	is distressed, runs to teacher with his hands over his ears, crying.
Anthony:	'I'm sorry, but you're going . . . it won't hurt you. You'll like to go up to the moon. You'll drop down in the nursery.'
Paul:	'I won't be a rocket. I don't want to be a rocket. I might not drop back into the nursery.' (Cries bitterly.)
Anthony:	'It's only pretend.' (With an affectionate gesture.)
Paul:	'All right then . . . it's only pretend. I haven't a hankey. It's fun. Everyone has to change into rockets.'
Anthony:	(to Simon) 'We need another two.'
Simon:	(shrinking): 'No.'
Paul:	'It's only pretend . . . You move about saying "gggh" and you drop back into the school. We're the best, aren't we, Anthony? . . . We go off lots . . . We're very big rockets. This is a hard game but we can do it. . . .'

This extract shows us just how vivid and frightening the imaginary world can be: Paul is afraid of being a rocket.

The game is *too* real; he is afraid that 'he will not drop back into the nursery again'. It is Anthony's reassurance that it is 'only pretend' that tips the scale for Paul. Only then can he begin to enjoy himself and is soon trying to persuade Simon to do likewise. So we can see at the beginning of the game that for Paul the edges of the real and imaginary world were blurred. He was just not sure what was what. 'It's only pretend' clarifies the situation for him and gives him courage.

Every time a child learns something about the world outside — how things work and what they are for — he is less at the mercy of the unknown, uncontrollable terrors which fill the world of fairy stories, myths and the religious beliefs of primitive peoples and seem to be a part of childhood. Many people believe that these fears are connected with the child's angry feelings towards those he loves. They suggest that the child has at times strong impulses of anger towards his mother or father when he would like to do something fairly violent. He then becomes afraid that these things might be 'done back to him' and it is certainly true that a child's world is very much 'an eye for an eye and tooth for a tooth' world, as anyone can see. These fears of retribution get pinned on to particular objects sometimes, and as we all know, a young child tends to see 'things' or 'objects' as having a life of their own. We say to a little child who has fallen down: '. . . naughty floor . . . smack the floor.' When we say this, we are tacitly admitting that in the child's mind it was the floor that came up and hit him. Most of us can remember objects in our bedroom at night which took on a sinister life of their own when the light was out. Gradually in the first years of life, the child begins to understand what we would call 'the reality' of these objects — that the flapping curtain is 'just a curtain' and

C

that it is the wind that makes it flap. Or, to take another example, children are often frightened by the business of going to the lavatory and learning about the way to work it themselves—pulling the chain and so on—can be a great help in overcoming fears. Though, in the long run, the child is reassured by knowledge, for periods of time panics about particular things may be too strong for reason.

All that begins to sound, however, as if imagination had only to do with fears; in fact, fears are only a small part of imagination. If we look back at Anthony's trip to the moon, we see clearly that the dreams of yesterday are the achievements of today; this is literally true in the particular instance of journeys to the moon. Without the power of imagination freely flowing, individuals and the human race could not progress; so imagination is precious and needs to be fostered; but it has to be balanced by a grasp of the reality outside, otherwise it is overwhelming to the child.

If you watch little children at play you will see the outer and the inner world work together and flow into one another all the time. Thus a piece of wood may be a dagger, a spade, and a magic wand all within a few moments, but if you say to the child: 'that's a nice dagger', he may reply: 'don't be silly, that's a piece of wood.' Never again will the edges be so blurred; this is partly what makes these first years so fascinating to study; it is the third major achievement of the ordinary child at about five years that he has begun to put together the outside and the inside worlds and make sense of them, using each in the service of the other.

How does the child achieve all this?

Growth and learning, physical, mental and emotional

never go forward steadily. They always proceed by fits and starts. As every mother knows, there are considerable variations between children in the age at which they do certain things — even the ordinary landmarks of sitting up, walking and talking. This is even more noticeable in those complicated matters of emotional development which I have been writing about. Nevertheless, the fact remains that at five years old, most children go to school and manage school life fairly well. What does that imply? It implies amongst other things that they have learnt to be sociable — up to a point; they can play together, share things and make friendships — they value themselves and other people. They can be apart from their mothers for most or all of the day and not be *too* frightened by this; yet they go charging home for tea and like it best if their mother is there. They can separate and belong at the same time. They can enter into learning about the outside world with great enthusiasm, as any good primary school teacher knows; yet they can turn happily to a make-believe world in playtime. The mixture is a rich one. So however different the children may be in the ways and the times that they achieve things, however differently they behave, by and large they emerge at about five ready to face new worlds outside the family.

Yet the achievement is not a steady constant one. Within the hour, the three-year-old may have given up a precious toy to her little brother and hit him with a spade. In May, the two-and-a-half-year-old is clean and dry. In June he is wet and dirty again. The child of two-and-a-half is screaming :do it myself' at one moment and the next moment he is wanting to be fed at mealtimes. The child of four is outside playing daring games and dashing in to demand a drink for himself and all his friends, until he hurts himself. Then he is two again, sitting on his mother's lap sucking his thumb. On Monday, we can explain to the three-year-old that the Hoover couldn't suck him into itself — only the dirt on the carpet — and he says brightly: 'I'm too big, aren't I?' We think he has seen reason but on Tuesday he is frightened of it again.

It is a matter of two steps forward and (usually) one step back. That is to say, where there has been solid achievement it is rarely completely lost, although to worried parents, it must sometimes seem like that. Of course, when the child's world is disturbed, progress is even more shaky — but that is what the next chapter is about.

If the world of the family is secure the child fights his inner battles more successfully. Without thinking about it ordinary parents are reliable enough. They are steady in their loving (which does *not* mean that they cannot be angry); in their discipline; in their attitudes to all sorts of things. They are the rocks. He can hang on to them, climb on them, throw stones at them and they are still there. He can't budge them.

Although it is right in our society to place the parents with the child at the centre of the first years' achievements, many other people contribute to the success of the first years, and when homes are broken they may play an even more vital part. Brothers and sisters and other playmates; uncles and aunts, friends and neighbours, nursery school teachers and — sometimes most important of all — grandparents, all or some of these can be key people. In some countries, little children are looked after by all sorts of relations and the care is not concentrated in the hands of the parents as we do. We should not overlook the way in which other people can help to 'spread the load' so that the intensity of the child's feelings about his parents can be lightened a little.

All this, however, is about relationships; there are other ways in which the child is helped to grow up. One of these is through play which is of central importance to the young child's development. Play has many uses. One of them I have already referred to—it helps the child to make a bridge between the real and the imaginary worlds. Here are some others:

1. The child works out in play what the grown up's world is like and what it feels like to be grown up. This you can see clearly in the numerous games of 'mothers and fathers', 'weddings', etc., which have gone on from time immemorial.

2. The child expresses in play his feelings about all kinds of situations, especially in the family, and feels better for it. For example, he smacks the doll for having a dirty bottom when he himself is trying not very successfully to be clean.

3. The child expresses in play his feelings about all are physical—climbing, hammering, and so on; some are mental—how things work, from bricks to jigsaws.

4. The child begins in play to co-operate with other children in various kinds of activity; he makes great strides in this between the years of three and five.

Everyone now knows that for all these reasons and others besides, we must give our little children opportunities to play. Good parents in some areas are very worried at the lack of such opportunities. Nursery schools and play groups are not a luxury but a necessity in some parts of the country, for instance where blocks of high flats make informal contact between children difficult.

The developing power of speech is of course another vital factor in these achievements I have been writing about. In the making of relationships, in many kinds of learning, in the relief of pressures inside of fear or anxiety, speech is of central importance. The speed at which the vocabulary increases between the ages of three and five is quite remarkable, and indeed learning to put a name to an object is in itself an amazing phenomenon which is in part responsible for the advances made by the human race compared with other animals. Ordinary parents never give a thought to this as they talk to their wordless babies or patiently repeat the names of things to their incoherent toddlers, but experience with deaf children or with children deprived of ordinary 'chat' in their early years, shows how greatly the developing child depends on speech for much of his progress.

What have they in common?

Ordinary little children come in all shapes and sizes; large and small, fat and thin, bright and dim, easy and difficult. But there is a common factor and it is difficult to find one word to describe it adequately. They are busy; they live life very intensely — in some ways more than at any other time. Sensations are vivid; the feeling of things like peaches or velvet or grain in a bucket; the smells of things like bonfires or people like grandma. When they are happy there isn't a cloud in the sky; when they are sad, the whole world is black. When they are happy it is for ever; when they are sad, it is for ever. They do not know that each will pass in time — when that lesson is learnt both kinds of feeling become less acute. They are interested in everything, and the everyday things of the world that we take for granted are a perpetual wonder. I am not saying that ordinary children must be ceaselessly active. As Winnicott remarks: 'Some children are never allowed even in earliest infancy just to lie back and float.'* But when the little child goes quiet and stares into space, you may be sure his head is not empty but full of rich dreams.

As long as excitement and vitality are flowing freely, there is nothing much to worry about. The six-year-old boy writing about his little sister somehow seems to convey the feeling better than grown-up words — perhaps because he is nearer to it.

> Our Jane is two
> She plays with a boy and
> She has white hair and
> She has blue eyes and
> She has a runny nose and
> She can't talk and
> She's fat and
> She pinched my biscuits and
> She's got a bike like an old cronk and
> She plays with my train and
> She's a monkey when telly's on:
> She plays about.
> She plays up and down.
> They let her. †

Some useful books

J. and E. Newson, *Patterns of Infant Care*, Penguin, 1971.

J. and E. Newson, *Four Years Old in an Urban Community*, Penguin, 1976.

(Studies over a number of years of how parents in Nottingham bring up their children.)

D. W. Winnicott, *The Child, the Family and the Outside World*, Penguin, 1964.

* Op. cit., p. 28.

† From A. B. Clegg, ed., *The Excitement of Writing*, Chatto & Windus, 1964.

(An important account of how families interact, based upon radio talks.)

H. Jolly, *Book of Child Care: the Complete Guide for Today's Parents*, Allen & Unwin, 1975.

S. Millar, *The Psychology of Play*, Penguin, 1968.

3 Foster children

Most of this chapter is about toddlers, not babies. This is because I do not think anyone can help foster parents very much in a book with their feelings about babies or with the babies' feelings about them. Good foster parents will do instinctively what the baby needs; you will handle him firmly but gently; you will find out what his particular rhythm of feeding is and adapt yourself to it; in short you will behave towards him as you would towards your own, except that you may not have quite the same specially sharpened awareness of his feelings and moods as the ordinary mother has after she has given birth. Still many foster parents seem to be able to re-create even this when they take a baby, just as couples do who have a baby placed with them for adoption. Of course, there may be times when you need special advice about the physical care of a baby: doctors or health visitors are the people to consult about this.

However, as I mentioned in the last chapter, it is quite helpful for foster parents to think a bit about the stages a baby goes through and when. If, as some people suggest, at *about* six months, babies are starting to recognise 'whole people' and there are the tiny, sensitive beginnings of concern for somebody besides himself, then obviously, although the baby cannot tell you in words, the first year of life is a difficult time for him to move from one person's care to another and, if this happens, he is likely to be confused and muddled for a time. We need a lot more observation from people like foster parents about the reactions of babies from about five to ten months to a move, especially when it is to good, loving ordinary care. We know beyond any doubt that lack of warm constant care is distressing and sometimes damaging to the child but foster parents could help a great deal to increase our understanding of the effect of the actual separation, as distinct from poor care. Here is one example which might seem to indicate that even at six months, there are deep and complicated things going on in the baby.

Joan was six months when she was placed with prospective adopters. She was a small but healthy baby who had spent the first six months of her life with her mother, who was hoping to marry the father and unable to decide about having Joan adopted. Eventually, she agreed to adoption and Joan was placed having been with her mother for six anxious, worried months. She had taken her feeds reasonably normally during that time, however, judging by her weight. On arrival, she gazed wistfully about her with large dark blue eyes; and went on what could justly be called a hunger-strike. She did not cry much, just lay and stared sadly at her adoptive parents. She lost weight eating practically nothing; doctors could find nothing the matter with her and the adoptive mother began to wonder if she would just fade away and die. Then, gradually, she began to take food but eating remained a problem right through childhood, with a tendency to be depressed and apathetic even in adult life.*

* Babies are now generally placed for adoption before they are six months old.

Many examples can, of course, be cited of babies who did not react so violently to a change of care. Clearly, we cannot discount the variations shown in different children according to constitution and heredity. The important thing to remember is that once the beginnings of relationships have been established, when and how we move children is of great importance and it may well be that these beginnings are a lot earlier than people used to think. As the baby cannot speak, it is up to the foster parents to watch him to try to understand what is going on. In this way you will be able to help him a little bit more. So much for babies. Now what about the toddlers — the child from one to four years old?

How does he see the foster parents?

You have been waiting for him, perhaps for weeks, perhaps for only a few hours; during that time you have pictured him and his arrival in your minds. But how is he seeing you? How does a little child see the grown-ups around him? We cannot remember but we can try and guess — so that we can understand his point of view better when he arrives. It is, after all, a very small point of view. You must seem so big: he has to lift his head to see your face. The writer Laurie Lee describes how he felt when he was about three years old.* He was frightened and felt lost in the long grass which he saw 'towering above me and all around me'. His sisters came to find him and they had 'huge shining faces hung up like shields between me and the sky'. The poet Lawrence Durrell, † writing of a baby, speaks of fingers which seem like 'beanstalks',

* Laurie Lee, *Cider with Rosie*. A lively autobiography of childhood in a Gloucestershire village.
† 'Clouds of Glory', in Lawrence Durrell, *Collected Poems*.

'chins like balconies' and 'kisses like blank thunder'.
So — you are big and you are powerful. You can pick him
up so that he is helpless and his legs dangle. We may
remember that feeling with our own parents — that they
were very strong and very powerful. This is both a
comfort and a worry to the child. It is a comfort because
it means it does not all depend on him: he does not have
to manage everything: but it is a worry because it makes
him feel so helpless and powerless sometimes. It must be
specially worrying for the little foster child, to whom all
this is a puzzle and a mystery. In his own home, he was
just getting to know where he was; to get some kind of
feeling of control over the world within his home — where
things were kept, how to use some of them, the way the
cupboard opened or the chair pulled. And of course, he
knew the people — their tones of voice, their looks — even
their smell. Now, suddenly, it is all unknown and it must
be rather like being put down in a foreign town with all
the signposts removed. Where *are* things — and rooms?
The lavatory makes a different noise and the bath is
huge. Worst of all, the people are new. Now he may of
course have met you before and if he has this is very
helpful. But even if he has, his memory is not the same as
ours would be; for one thing, the younger the child, the
less able he will be to hold the picture of you in his mind
for any length of time. For another, as we all know,
feeling worried and afraid can somehow blur the picture
of the real person so that they do not look the same.
When you are standing there in the hall, perhaps feeling
all warm and motherly, he *may* be seeing you as a bit
witch-like and wicked, for as we have seen in chapter 2,
his imaginary world may not be at all like the reality.
Children we know are fascinated by fairy stories of
witches and especially by the stories of wicked grown-ups

deceiving children. Red Riding Hood finds her grandmother is really the wolf dressed up. These old fairy stories would have died a long time ago if they did not strike a chord in the child somewhere. Somewhere, in the little child's imaginings, grown-ups are at times frightening, even a bit sinister. We often hear laughter turning to a scream of fear when grown-ups are playig with the children. Now if this is true for all children, it is going to be even more so for the foster child when he is faced with these unfamiliar people who want to do things to him — wash him, change his clothes and so on.

So, when this child you are going to look after comes into your house, try and take a 'child's eye view' and imagine what it might be like for him. You will get clues from him to help you understand — but I will write more about this presently. Of course, a great deal will depend on what his experience of adults has been up till then; the more affection he has given and received, the easier your job will be because he will be expecting love and go out to you more easily to get it. But it is important to remember that whether he has been much loved or neglected, this break in his life is a big strain for him and a bit of him must see you and your home as frightening — even if he does not show it at first.

How is he feeling?

What, then, can you, the foster parents, expect in those days, weeks or months he is with you? One thing you can be sure of is that he is going to be rather muddled and mixed up in his feelings. If what follows sounds rather gloomy, as if learning about a foster child was all 'problems' rather than fun, this is only because I am taking the fun for granted. From the last chapter it is clear that there is great enjoyment in getting to know this age of child, and after all, foster parents will not need help in this. The happy easy times will be there with your foster children as with your own. But there may also be difficult times when you are puzzled, and worried, by the things that seem to be happening between you and your foster child. So let us turn to this side of things.

The first thing to say is that if you are lucky, he will cry. That may sound strange but after all it is natural for him to be upset in this situation and equally natural for him to show it. This is not an age when we expect children to bottle up their feelings. If he can be open about it, it means he has something to be sad about — that he grieves for his parents and his home, though, of course, he may not be able to show it for a while. So there is no need to worry about tears and he should be given a chance to cry — not be 'cheered up' too quickly. We can all feel better after a good cry.

But these tears will not only be sad tears; they will be angry ones too. All children are angry at times — this I have said is healthy for it means they are asserting themselves as people. But a foster child may have a special kind of anger, because he feels he has been let down by those who should have been reliable. There may have been very good reasons — his mother had to go to hospital and his father could not stay at home from work — but in the child's mind this is desertion. For at this stage of his life, he feels the world ought to be circling round him. And, in a way, he is right, for the ordinary child does take for granted that his world, his family, will stay the same and that he will for a time be the centre of attention. The faith of the foster child has been shaken. So he is angry, but he is also worried in case it is his fault, his naughtiness which sent his mother away or removed him from his home. We know that even older children who have been away from their parents a long time will say that they did something to deserve it — it was their badness, even when there is no truth whatever in this. The little child cannot grasp the complicated reasons for the break up — temporary or permanent — of his home. So if his mother goes to hospital, it may be in his mind that it was because he was naughty or bold and made her ill. Even an everyday phrase — 'You've made Mummy tired' may suddenly have a new meaning if he is told later — 'Mummy is tired and she has gone away for a rest.'

So, he may be sad, angry, guilty, all at the same time and this is not a nice feeling inside. This is very hard on you, the foster parents, because of course, you are not responsible for what happened before. But he has to show you these feelings and find out that you will stand them and go on caring for him before he can really believe in you, believe that you will not desert him as he feels he was deserted before.

However, there are many children who cannot show their feelings right away. This is a pity because experience has shown that sooner or later they will, and it might as well be sooner! It is as if these children can only cope with the situation by pretending nothing has happened. Often such children are very good for quite a long time and give no trouble.

Linda was two-and-a-half when she came to her foster home, a large fair child with long hair and blue eyes. The foster mother commented that she was no trouble and even on the first night she did not cry when left. She ate everything, was dry and clean.

She did not cry at all, but the foster mother said it was a bit unnatural and she was too controlled. Her one fault seemed to be bossiness, for Linda tried to control everyone around her, making them play the games she wanted in her own way. This went on for two months and then she was ill with tonsilitis. Children naturally become more babyish when they are ill but Linda became extremely so. She became very dependent on the foster mother, and very demanding. She would cling on to her — not liking her to go to the lavatory or outside without her. She wept for no apparent reason. This went on for about three weeks and at the end of the time she gradually became less clinging — but also less bossy and managing. From then on she began to be really 'one of the family'. Her bossiness seemed to be part of her need to 'keep a grip on everything', including herself. Once she had let herself go and been miserable and babyish, she could relax and begin to make a real relationship with the family and in particular the foster mother.

Children may have all kinds of ways of hiding from their foster parents and perhaps also from themselves, what they are really feeling and needing. They may be like Linda — too independent and too bossy. They may, like Linda, need an illness — perhaps not a very serious one — to help let themselves go. Or perhaps, like Elizabeth, some event in the foster family will crack the shell their foster child has been putting over her feelings.

Elizabeth was eighteen months when fostered. She was brown eyed and square and seemed a bit stolid. Like Linda she gave no trouble at all for quite a while; 'the perfect child', even dry and clean at this young age. Five months after she went to the foster parents, her foster brother, aged ten, went to hospital for a few days and when he came back he naturally got quite a lot of attention. Then and not till then, did Elizabeth show her feelings. She dirtied herself and she had crying fits; as the foster mother said, 'more like a tantrum but with nothing to have a tantrum about'. But Elizabeth *did* have something to have a tantrum about. She had been the youngest in this foster family and very much the centre of attention. When the attention was diverted — even slightly and temporarily from her — she showed that she was not really secure yet by this outburst of feeling: the crying fits persisted for some time. The foster mother said she would cry for cake 'even when she did have some on her plate'. She wanted to have her cake and eat it.

The stories of Linda and Elizabeth show that once the breakthrough has come and the children are able to show you how much they need you, they are going to be afraid they will lose you as they 'lost' the other adults. A period can therefore be expected when they are clinging, worried at letting you out of their sight. 'Seeing is believing', we say; and for little children it is the only way they can be sure the foster parents are still there.

How can you understand him?
Every good parent understands a great deal of what is going on in a child, without putting it into words. He knows it because he was once a child and there are half-hidden memories to help him understand. But being a foster parent may require a bit of extra understanding and knowledge both of the child and of yourself in order to help him more. For although we all have the same *kinds* of feelings — of love and anger, of sadness and happiness and so on, children and adults who have suffered a lot may have a different *mixture* of these

D

feelings and different ways of showing them. So it is worth while trying to observe and notice more closely what is going on in foster children than you would ordinarily do with your own children. In the rush and bustle of a working day — when there are a hundred other things to do — it is very easy to miss the clues which the child gives us to how he is feeling.

The young child's day is spent mainly in three ways; either he is playing, or he is sleeping, or he is taking part in the ordinary family activities — eating, washing, and so on.

In some ways, play can help us most in understanding the child and yet it may be the part of the child's day we notice least because it does not affect us as much as his other activities, unless he is actually playing with the grown-ups. It is easier to notice what is going on once he has learnt to talk and we hear the running commentaries as he plays. But long before the words are there, the child's play has a meaning and a purpose, and play will have the same kind of importance to a foster child as it does to the ordinary child (see chapter 2). You can learn about your foster child in two ways — *how* he plays and *what* he plays.

It is not surprising if a child, who has had all kinds of unsettling experiences and is upset about them, is pretty rough with his toys. We all sometimes turn our anger on to the thing that is small or cannot hit back. So you need not be upset if nice new toys are broken and spoilt, or if the doll is beaten hard for being naughty. Probably it is best to wait a while before providing toys that are at all expensive and give him instead the kinds of toy with which he can safely be angry — after all, it is a harmless enough outlet!

You may also notice that when children first come to

your home they are either too still or too busy. Most of us have a tendency to go in one direction or another when we are anxious or afraid; we either get very quiet and try to look as if we were not there; or else we get very busy and dash about—cleaning all the house, for instance. The same may happen with the foster child; he may hold back, afraid to play; Linda was like this on some days; on other days she seemed to be playing busily but if you looked closely, you saw it was somehow not true. Linda walked stiffly and awkwardly. Her voice was gruff and stilted. She never let her imagination flow freely—if you read her a story and asked her 'what happened then' she said 'nothing' and closed the book. After her illness and growing attachment to the foster mother all this began to change—her voice and walk became more natural and she began to play much more openly.

On the other hand, your foster child might be like Sally.

> Sally was two when fostered, a little fair haired girl with a clownish face. When I first visited, she was ceaselessly on the move. She would run in and out of the house, seizing all kinds of toys and objects, playing with them for a brief moment and passing on to something else, throwing them down. She seemed to pay very little attention to the grown-ups round her. Gradually, as the weeks went by, she concentrated better on playing with the same things and began to show toys to the grown-ups.

This of course is another important point. For little children have half an eye on the grown-ups while they are playing and want to involve them in their games. We can learn about them from this too. Sally began by ignoring the grown-ups altogether; then she began to offer us toys but would snatch them away as we stretched out a hand to them with a loud 'no'. Then she began to leave them in our laps for quite a long while. All this was a sign of her gradually increasing trust in her new world.

So much then can be learnt from how children play: but what they play is also important. For instance, when you are trying to get your children clean, you will often notice they love to play with water or with dark soft substances — earth, Plasticine, paints and so on, and this is of course the same for foster children too. Sally was for ever picking up small round knobs of earth, saying 'dirty' and flinging them away. At that time she was having quite a struggle to keep clean; and it is easy to see the connection between this and her games. Understanding play is a complicated business and we must leave it to the experts to unravel the deeper meaning of children's play. But there are times when the meaning is not far to seek, especially with children who have had a difficult time.

> Timothy, three years old, was playing with his toy soldiers, and they were always being blinded in the battles and rushed off to hospital. This boy's father had had trouble with his eyes and there was a risk he might go blind. The little boy had showed very little feeling openly about this but in his play he showed clearly enough his anxiety about his father. It helped him, of course, to 'play it out' for the soldiers got better in hospital, and it was a safe way of bringing his fears into the open.

You can also learn a bit about how the child sees his family life from what he plays. His games of 'mothers and fathers', for example, tell you something about his picture of the home he has come from. But a word of warning here — his imagination colours the picture. For instance, you cannot assume because John is hitting his teddy hard and saying 'naughty' that he has actually been beaten. It may be that he *feels* he has been a naughty boy and he is really smacking himself. The important thing is for the foster parents to try to understand how *he* sees his family; it may be vastly different from how you would see it.

But of course he does not only play. He sleeps, he eats, he uses (or does not use) his pot and he spends a great deal of time with you, in different situations. So what of these?

Somewhere in the back of our minds, we may perhaps have a picture of an ideal, happy toddler, who sleeps soundly at nights, who eats heartily, who is slowly but surely getting clean and dry and so on. Those who have had their own children know that no such child exists. All children have phases of bad behaviour, or of being upset; of bad dreams and night terrors, of picking at food and wanting biscuits between meals, of wetting just as soon as they come off the pot. So of course foster children will be like this too — only probably more so.

Christopher was two and a half when he was fostered — a brown eyed plump little boy whose skin and teeth were in poor condition from a diet of cider and chips. He used to wake up at nights from what seemed to be a nightmare and the foster mother found it took a long time before he came round — he would sit up stiffly, staring into space as if he could not shake off the dream. Often at nights he would ask for all the doors to be left open and seemed really terrified if they were closed.

It is not difficult to feel sorry for Christopher about this — we can clearly see that he is in a state, that he has no control over such episodes. The foster parent's task gets harder, however, when the child shows his disturbance in every part of the day's activities—like Christopher, who would scream and kick his foster mother, throw his dinner at her, stuff toys down the lavatory and so on. Foster children are not usually as difficult as Christopher, but if you remember how very important the day-to-day business of eating and potting are, and how much the foster mother is involved in them with him, you will not be surprised if these activities are the cause of a good deal of trouble sometimes. A foster mother once said to me of an eighteen-month-old child: 'You know, I reckon food and love are the same thing to a child.' If you think of a baby, it is clear that you cannot separate food from love. The little child is very near still to the baby. As a matter of fact, this connection of food with love stays with us all our lives. It hurts us if anyone refuses the food we have spent a long time preparing, and we all feel 'loved' when people remember what we like to eat. Don't we say 'the way to a man's heart is through his stomach'? If your foster child is not sure yet about taking love from the new adults in his life, he may show it most at meal times—and he may show it in various ways, depending partly on what he has experienced in the past and partly on the kind of child he is. He may eat ravenously. At first you will be pleased; then you may wonder if it is not too much of a good thing—this constant stuffing. Or he may fidget or fuss until you could scream, using meal-times to demand from you a great deal of attention. Or he may just seem not hungry for a time, as if there were no enjoyment in eating. Children brought up by their own parents show this kind of variation; but with the foster child these difficulties may, at times, be especially marked and it may be easier to understand them if they can be seen as all part of his struggle to manage the muddle he is in about being loved.

The same applies to getting him clean and dry. As I have said in the first chapter, all ordinary children have to learn to 'toe the line' and behave in ways that the grown-ups will like. Children get clean because they want to please the grown-ups and be like them. Your foster child may seem to be clean and dry when he first arrives in the foster home but it may be he has to, as it were, start all over again with you and decide that he wants to please you. This may really be quite an effort for he may feel that his motions are something of his very own (and after all, he has not brought very much of his own with him) or being wet may remind him of when he was a baby—it was a nice warm feeling when he did it and he wishes he could still be a baby. So these things may take longer to get right than with ordinary children.

The really important thing in all this is that it is all bound up with you, the foster mother: he is not eating food, he is eating your food: he is not just using his pot, he is using it for you. It is not the single bits of behaviour that matter but how they all add up in helping you to understand how he is feeling about you.

We all accept that the mother is of very great importance—probably the greatest importance—to the very small child. But when young children come to a foster home, they sometimes seem 'all for Dad'. This is flattering for Dad but a bit upsetting for Mum.

Elizabeth had been in her foster home for about two months when this incident occurred. She was in the room with a Social Worker and me. She picked up a bag of sweets. The Social Worker said, 'Give them to Mummy.' She paused, trotted over and gave them to me. I said, 'Give them to Mummy.' She took them and gave them to the Social Worker, who said: 'There's Mummy, in the kitchen.' She then went into the kitchen with the sweets. On the same visit, she brought a book to me. She pointed to a picture of a little boy and said 'baby' several times. Then to the man, saying 'Dad, dad'. On the same page there was a picture of a woman; she ignored it and would not answer when I said: 'Who's that? . . .'

I think these two incidents show us that a part of Elizabeth was shutting Mother out; Elizabeth could say the word 'Mummy' as she could say 'Dad' and 'baby' and many other words. But she was muddled, even angry, that the most important person in her world had vanished. (She had been with her own mother till she was nearly a year old, then spent some months in a residential nursery.) So she came to a dead stop at the idea of Mother, even after two months in her foster home. Elizabeth, according to her foster mother, was 'all for Dad' at first; so was Linda, until she was ill, when she turned to her foster mother with such desperate urgency. Linda would have none of her foster father while she was ill. Afterwards she was friends with him again but her love was more evenly shared between the parents. So it may sometimes happen that a child cannot take straightaway from a woman — another mother — what is offered. It is sometimes said when children come from a residential nursery to a foster home, that their enthusiasm for men is because they have lived in a 'world of petticoats'. Doubtless this plays its part but it is not the whole story; Linda, for example, had come from her own family, with men about. If these things are not understood, it is easy for foster parents to be hurt about it and maybe even a bit jealous of each other; the foster mother may feel rejected at first; the foster father may be bewildered when he goes out of favour. There is nothing really to be done except to wait your turn and help the child find a real normal balance in his relationships. He needs you both in different ways.

So far I have been making suggestions about different aspects of a child's activities and behaviour which may help foster parents to understand what is going on. But you do not, of course, just want to study your foster child; you want to help him to settle down happily for the time he is with you.

How can you help him?

It is obvious from what has been said so far that the beginning of helping is understanding—and it is not necessary always for foster parents to put that into words either to yourself or to him. Understanding of course will affect the way you handle all kinds of situations that crop up.

Sometimes the most important and deepest thing foster parents can do to help is to let the child start again as a baby with them. Let me explain what I mean. Some—though not all—foster children will not have had a good time when they were babies; they will not have had a close enough relationship with their mothers. In each new relationship they hope to find what they missed. For most of us who had a good enough time with our mothers when we were babies, it is somehow a part of us so that we do not have to go on looking and can give it to our children in turn. Some foster children will still be looking. Now this is difficult for you, the foster mother;

after all, perhaps he is two-and-a-half years not two-and-a-half weeks old; you may have a lot to do and a lot of other people to consider. He is not the only pebble on your beach, yet he wants to be. He may show it by his constant demands on you or by his resentment and jealousy of others, especially younger children. He may want to suck a bottle, though he is three years old. Even his wetting and soiling may be part of his wish to go back again. The foster child may be wanting to start again with you, in that deep exclusive relationship of ordinary mothers and new babies. It may be you cannot do this for him and if you cannot, it is not your fault. You cannot make up this kind of feeling. But if you feel this happening between the two of you, then it may be a very important thing and valuable and you should not try and stop yourself or worry about 'making him babyish'. He may have to go backwards before he can go forwards. But not every one of you who reads this bit will need to understand because not all foster children will ask this of their foster parents. It is perhaps important, too, to mention here that foster parents are human too — that they can only stretch themselves so far and give so much of themselves to someone else's child.

One of the most vital things which you can do is to help the child keep his past, his present and his future joined up. I suggested in the first chapter that the young child is struggling to establish himself as a person; it is very important therefore that he should not feel that his life is chopped up into pieces that somehow do not connect — and this is what deprived children often do feel. There is much that you can do to help over this, some of it very practical.

If you ask yourselves the question 'What is important to a child?' you will think of all sorts of things you want to find out before he comes. Of course, you will not always be able to get your questions answered — in an emergency for example — when the mother is not available to tell you or the social worker these vital details. But it is no harm to have an ideal, a standard, even if you cannot always reach it. So you will want to know, for instance, what sort of food he is used to, what words he uses for his pot and his motions, what time he is used to going to bed, and so on. Routine is very important to the little child and you can help him a lot by sticking as closely as possible to what he has been used to for a while, until you can gradually change him to your own ways, where that is necessary.

Then there is the matter of what he brings with him. Those foster parents who have had their own children, may have noticed that a piece of stuff or an old battered toy was often specially important to them and was carried everywhere. Usually, far back in the past, this had some link with mother — a piece of her nightie, for instance, that wore out and had to be replaced by something else. It is a very valuable object to the child because it is a kind of bridge between him and his mother. It is not his own body — his fingers or toes — but neither is it actually a part of his mother. So he can keep it with him, have it when he wants. It is in a way more reliable than mother. It is one of the child's ways of managing the conflict between wanting to be separate and wanting to belong which I discussed in the last chapter. Obviously, therefore, it is a very serious loss if a little child who has such an object is parted from it. It is a good idea for foster parents to enquire if he has one and to encourage the social worker to bring it. You may have to put up with a very dirty bit of blanket for a while, as he may not like the smell of it washed! Not all children have such 'cuddlies', not all are deeply attached to them. But for those who are, it is very important indeed to make sure they come with the child when he moves.

Of course, all possessions and clothes are significant to the little child; they are a part of him and they must be respected. This is easily forgotten when a ragged, grubby child arrives and the foster parents can buy or have bought for him a lovely set of new clothes. It is easy to feel he will be as thrilled as you are with a new rig-out. He may be, in time, but his old clothes are a part of him and of his past and if you have to make the change, it is a help to make it gradually and perhaps put the old tight jersey back on for a few days after it has been washed!

Another thing to think about is partings. When I was a social worker and took a small child to the foster home, sometimes with the mother, we sometimes funked the screams which would follow when the parents and I said we were going and the foster mother would divert the child's attention while we stole away. This saves the grown-ups the upset of hearing a child's distress but does it really help the child? Suddenly, mysteriously, the grown-ups disappear. You turn your back and they are gone. With so many muddles and confusions about what is happening, let us not add one more. The screams and the tears are better, because at least the child knows what happened—Mummy or Daddy went down the road, they did not just vanish into thin air. This is not to say that you should 'go on' too much about parting and prolong the agony. A fairly quick departure after perhaps one warning is better than long drawn out farewells.

Then there is the question of preparations—both for coming to the foster home and, in some instances, for leaving it. This varies a great deal according to the age of the child; less can be done for the eighteen-month-old than for the four-year-old because his remembering and understanding is not so good. Also it depends a lot on his intelligence, because a child of four who is not very intelligent may be needing the kind of explanation that would ordinarily be given to a two-year-old. Obviously it is a good thing if he can be prepared by seeing beforehand the people he is going to live with. It is best of all, if the foster parents can make friends with him in his own familiar world before he comes, or if his parents, who may have become strangers to him, can see him in the foster home before they have him back. This takes off some of the shock of strangeness which he must experience. The very little child cannot hold on to the picture of an adult very long, however, and it is no good imagining you have solved his problems of separation and change by these devices, though you may soften the blow a bit.

Equally important — or even more important — is talking with the child about the past and the future. You can do so much to help keep the memories alive which will make it easier for him when he goes home and if you know his parents and his family, this is much easier for you. This is another reason why, when possible, it is good for you to see his home. You can talk about the cat, or the budgie, the other children, and so on. You can try and get a snap of his parents and show it to him when you are talking together. You may discover he has all kinds of odd ideas about what has happened. For instance, Tommy, aged four, who was in a residential nursery, told a social worker: 'I 'spect Badenam [his home town] is in the pond.'* Tommy was really saying: 'My home has gone for ever — vanished; it isn't just that I have moved — it's the

* This illustration is from Clare Winnicott's article 'Casework in the Child Care Service', reprinted in *Child Care and Social Work*, Codicote Press, 1964.

town that has gone — to the bottom of the pond.' The social worker said to him: 'Because you have come away, it does not mean anything has happened to Badenham and your home is still waiting for you to go back to. . . .' Foster parents will think of all kinds of practical ways of helping him with his memories, but you should bear in mind the two things I have discussed earlier; first, he is not just forgetful, he is angry and hurt, and so he is deliberately shutting things out of his mind; second, he cannot understand what has happened in an adult way and so he will have strange imaginings and pictures of his home and his mother. You may have to find these feelings out before you can really help him by explaining the truth.

If you have been talking to him all along about his family and home, then much of the work preparing him for the return is done. But you will still have to think about what you should say about actually going home. It is easy to overdo this. To keep saying to a two-and-a-half-year-old — 'In two weeks — in one week — in two days' time — you will be going home' may well make him more anxious and puzzled since he has not sufficient sense of time to grasp the meaning. A few hours may seem an eternity — what about weeks? Of course, the older he gets the more possible it is, if he is normally intelligent. So you will have to decide with each individual child, taking into account his age and his intelligence, how much of this should be done. The vital thing is that he should be helped to see his life in as much of a whole as possible. This will be easier for you to do if you can accept that he has a past — and a future that may not be with you. If you can't accept it, then both of you may try to shut it out and in the long run this will lead to muddle and confusion.

Much of what I have said has assumed that your foster child will not be with you permanently. It is worth mentioning again that by far the greatest number of young children who come into care do so for short periods only—hence the emphasis of my remarks. This fact has been somewhat obscured by recent publicity over 'Tug-of-Love' situations, which, though tragic, are happily rare. Many foster parents take on the job, knowing and accepting that their caring will be for short periods—indeed, some prefer it that way. For such children, 'keeping his parents alive' is quite crucial. There are practical ways of doing this. For example, when the Robertsons* fostered young children, they used dolls to illustrate where Mummy was, in a hospital bed, Daddy at home, in the house, going out to work, the child in 'Aunty's House' and so on. Repeated games of moving the dolls to meet and to part were played and probably seemed much more real to the child than words.

It is more difficult to know how to use or keep awake memories of home when you are uncertain how long your foster child will be staying with you. Clearly, the balance is very difficult to strike and it has to be related to the age of the child. For example, at eighteen months, it may be virtually impossible to keep memories alive unless there is regular parental contact whereas, at three, many children have strong bonds of intense loyalty to their parents which can cause them to fight against becoming too fond of their foster parents.†

Perhaps in such situations, and in those in which the child may never go home, the important thing is your own feelings and attitudes about his past and his parents because your foster child will 'get the message' of how you

* James and Joyce Robertson's fostering films are described on p. 67.

† The Robertsons' films illustrate these age differences brilliantly.

are feeling. As I shall discuss later, this may have an important effect on his development, because it does not help him to feel his parents are condemned by others. It can make him feel worthless too.

Later in this book, I shall discuss some of the ways in which the parents of your foster child may have behaved towards him and some of the possible reasons. There are many things which puzzle and upset foster parents about a child's experiences in his own home. For the moment, I will only talk about the child himself and how he may appear when he comes to you.

Sadly, it is very unlikely that the children who come into your home will have a straightforward, stable family life. Most parents have relatives and friends who will care for their children in short-term emergencies. So even short periods in care may indicate that the parents are in some kind of difficulty. Therefore, your foster child may not simply react as any ordinary child to separation from loved ones, for example, by being distressed, angry and difficult for a time. The sad thing is that the child who is most disturbed, whose behaviour is the oddest, may be the one whose relationship with his own parents is least satisfactory. This is because he has not had the absolute security of his parents' love to start him off on his journey to a strange family. It would be quite wrong to suggest that most children who are fostered have not been loved by their parents. But often the parents' own life has been full of stress and strain, such as poor housing, poverty, loneliness and broken marriages and this is bound to affect the way they behave towards their children.

There is one group of children about whom we hear a great deal in the papers these days — those who have been physically ill-treated or neglected by their parents. I must emphasise that, whatever the publicity, they form only a tiny proportion of young children received into care. It would be most unhelpful if foster parents became automatically suspicious of children's parents. Nevertheless, it is important to observe a child's physical condition and behaviour carefully when he arrives. He will, of course, have a medical examination but you, as foster parents, can play your part. There are a variety of physical signs, of which the most obvious is bruising. But do remember that children tumble about; the age of the child and the kind of bruising are crucial in deciding the cause. If you are worried you should contact your social worker *at once*, because bruises quickly fade. However, in most cases this will have been noticed at the medical examination.

Another possible symptom is, of course, excessive thinness. There is a condition known as 'failure to thrive' and it is not often a simple matter of the child being starved. Sometimes, a peculiar interaction exists between mother and child so that the child is fed the wrong kind of food and/or rejects the food he is offered. Bearing in mind that children's weight at the same age varies considerably, you may nevertheless be on occasions alarmed at how thin he is. If this is directly due to the situation at home, when he has been with you a while, he should begin to gain weight. Never forget, however, that there might be a physical cause and that children, like adults, may go off their food when they are unhappy for whatever reason. None the less, if you are fostering temporarily, and you were seriously perturbed by the child's physical appearance when he came to you, it is important to tell your social worker before the time comes for him to return. Incidentally, the condition of a child's clothes is not necessarily significant *either way*. He may be beautifully turned out yet physically ill-treated; he

E

may be very scruffy by your standards and come from a warm, tender home.

There is one other sign which might put you on your guard; doctors call it 'frozen watchfulness'. If a child is unnaturally still and watches you continuously, perhaps flinching if you go near, that is worrying and, again, you should tell your social worker. At the same time, foster parents have to learn from experience to distinguish between perfectly ordinary shyness with strangers, which sometimes includes shrinking away if you go to pick him up, and a symptom caused by serious physical ill-treatment.

I have been suggesting a few warning signs: of course, there are others, but it is essential that you consult with social workers, health visitors, doctors and so on, if you are worried, *because it is the accumulation of information, not isolated signs*, which may provide the necessary evidence to suggest a child should not go home or will have to be carefully supervised at home. Children must not be snatched away from their parents; how would you feel? And all of us at present have to keep a sense of proportion so that we are not imagining signs of physical ill-treatment.

Nowadays foster parents are increasingly being asked to foster young children who are 'different' in one of two ways. First, they may be handicapped, physically or mentally. Second, they may be of different race or of mixed racial background. Although everything that has so far been said applies to all foster children, there are some special points to bear in mind if you are considering taking one of these children into your home.

Handicapped children
If you foster a young child who is handicapped, it is quite

likely that he will have been in residential care or hospital
before coming to you, since his handicap may have been
the reason for his reception into care. Most residential
nurseries or hospitals provide excellent physical care and
there are many devoted nurses but it is extremely difficult
to provide adequate 'parenting' in such establishments —
hence the fact you are asked to foster these children. This
means that some (not all) who come to you have, in a
sense, an emotional handicap as well, because they have
not experienced normal family life and continuous
relationships. Unfortunately, this can have an effect on a
child's intellectual and physical development. For
example, as I have mentioned earlier, play is a vital
ingredient in stimulating children mentally. If over-
pressed nurses have not been able to provide enough of
this, the child may appear more retarded than he would
in a normal environment. Similarly, if he is physically
handicapped, careful opportunities for 'adventuring'
may help him to overcome it to some extent. But this
means constant vigilance by the adult and may not be
easy to achieve in a busy nursery.

So it is important that you approach your task with
hope, knowing that your foster child may catch up in
some ways remarkably quickly. But it is vitally important,
at the same time, that you are realistic about what you
can achieve, given the nature of the handicap. I would
advise any foster parent who is considering taking a
seriously handicapped child to ask the social worker for
an appointment with a specialist doctor, probably a
paediatrician, to see what you may reasonably expect at
different ages and stages. That way you will spare
yourself painful disappointment, and most important,
you will not place upon your foster child this burden of
false hopes, which is very different from optimism.

In chapter 2, I described the way in which a child strives to belong and at the same time to be separate. This is a key struggle in the early years for all children. For a handicapped child and those who care for him, it is bound to pose some special problems. There is no denying his difference from ordinary children. There are some things they simply cannot do or can only do with much greater effort. Therefore, it is very difficult for all concerned to get the proper balance between dependence and independence at the different stages. Take toilet training, for example, which is a universal and crucial stage in child development. The handicapped child may have practical difficulties in managing this, or he may be slower than average: or he may never be able to control bowel or bladder, or both. Whether he is physically or mentally handicapped, he will almost certainly experience this as embarrassing or shameful or humiliating or all three. He will recognise himself as somehow different, unless he is grossly mentally handicapped (and few foster parents would feel able to take on such children). Common sense and kindness go a long way. But unless you have had previous experience of such work, it seems highly desirable that you should have on-going contact with experts, such as health visitors, with whom you can discuss progress and problems and also to have mutual support of groups concerned with the care of such children. The goal is to enable the handicapped child to lead as normal a life as possible. But this is not achieved by denying limitations. And, in different ways, he is bound to remain more dependent on you than ordinary children. On the other hand, it may be desirable (though hard) for foster parents sometimes to let such a child struggle longer to solve a problem in his own time, rather than rush to help.

There can be no greater contribution to child welfare than to provide a stable, normal family life for a handicapped child. But it is important to think about the effects this may have on your family relationship and especially upon your own children. These I shall discuss in chapter 5.

At first glance, it seems ridiculous, even perhaps rather insulting, to follow such a discussion with reference to children of different race from the foster parents. They are not handicapped in the same sense at all. But there are two important points to consider.

Children of different race

First, some (not all) will come to foster parents from their own parents. Some years ago, for example, quite large numbers of African children were placed privately with foster parents in the south-east of England because their parents were students (studying desperately, incidentally, for the education which we take for granted). Some such children had been used to a completely different family life, perhaps a big group of relations sharing in their care, certainly different food and so on. As a foster parent, you always need to learn something of this child's background. But when a child comes from your own society, you probably take a lot for granted which you have to make an effort to discover when a child comes from another, far-off, country. This is not, of course, to do with his colour, as such. The same would apply if he came from Turkey or Israel. But it happens that most of our foster children from different countries and cultures are of another colour. (One minor point which *is* relevant to colour is knowing when he is 'off-colour'!)

If a coloured child is to live with you for a long time or

permanently, the second vital point is how he feels about this difference in appearance from those he grows to love. I well remember an adopted relative (who was not coloured) looking round the table and saying suddenly, 'Why am I the only one in this room with brown eyes?' This, I believe, was not only a question, it was a sudden, not very happy, realisation of *difference*. We accept, unthinkingly, so much similarity ('he is just like his Uncle Jack'); and one often hears of adopted children, who are said to look remarkably like their adoptive relations. This simply cannot be when your foster child is black, brown or yellow, with features unlike your own! This may eventually seem unimportant in comparison with the bonds and similarities of interests, attitudes and so on, which hold you together. But I would hazard a guess that there is no coloured foster child, who loves his white foster parents, who will not at some time sorrow at, or resent, the difference between them. This, then, is your challenge, as foster parents; to face the difference with your foster child and, above all, to help him feel his colour is as good as yours. This, sadly, is far easier said than done. There are tragic, and not uncommon, stories of black children in care scrubbing their faces to make them white. As foster parents, you live in a society where there is still prejudice and unkindness towards coloured people. The young child is frequently admired, even fussed over; he is 'cute'. But there is a hard road ahead for him and if his early years with you are good, he will have the strength to bear it. There are practical ways of helping him to cope from an early stage. For example, there are books now written by West Indians for West Indian children, which tell of their history and way of life at home. What about pictures or posters in the house which show the child from an early age that many others look like him? But above all, open discussion of physical characteristics as the child begins to notice them is an acknowledgment of a difference of which there is nothing to be ashamed, perhaps especially if he is 'half and half' since then it may be harder still to know where he belongs.

When is there cause for worry?

I have discussed earlier some causes for worry about the child's own family life. But some of you will be keeping children for a long time or permanently so that this particular worry does not arise. It is difficult to give firm advice as to when to worry! We know that all normal children in their own homes have periods when they are upset and naughty and that these pass in time. You will, therefore, be expecting the same, only more so, of your foster children. But you may come up against kinds of difficult behaviour you have not met before which may take much longer to pass than with your own. I cannot even say that you 'should worry if after so many months he is still doing it', for children vary greatly in speed which they settle down in somebody else's home and the improvement will not be steady and even.

There are, however, a few things to take seriously and about which you should seek expert advice if after a while they do not come right. First, if your foster child seems apathetic or withdrawn over a fairly long period of time. This obviously follows from the description in chapter 2 of the 'common factor' which ordinary little children share of excitement and wonder. If this is missing, he cannot progress as does the ordinary child. If your foster child stays 'numb', that could be an indication that bodes ill for the future, that he is emotionally ill or mentally retarded.

Second, you may ask yourself: 'What is going on between him and me?' If something is going on—if you are sometimes cross with each other, sometimes fond, this is live, real relationship. But if you feel that in spite of him being perhaps very active there is a kind of hollow or emptiness in the child, that, try as you will, you can't like him because you feel he doesn't like anybody, then you should not hide this feeling from yourselves and others; you should admit to it and talk to someone who understands these problems. If the child you look after has had very many changes in his early life and has had really no chance to love anyone, he may be damaged in his feelings pretty badly. This does not mean you cannot make him better—you may be able to do so. But you may have to be prepared for a long uphill struggle and not all foster parents can undertake the task. If you cannot, it is best to admit to it sooner rather than later.

Some children go through a phase of fussiness over cleanliness when they are being toilet trained and are unnecessarily particular over all kinds of dirt—grubby hands or faces for example. This usually passes. If it does not pass, it is worth taking steps with a little child deliberately to help him to relax and get dirty and wet now and again, for example, through sand pits or water. If this is permitted, he will gradually let himself go and enjoy it—as ordinary children naturally do. If he is not helped about this, he might turn into the kind of 'pernickety' adult who simply has to have everything 'just so'. This kind of person is often not happy within himself and very tense to live with.

Similarly, most young children have periods when they become afraid of something, animals, the lavatory cistern, and so on. If, as a child grows to school age, these fears do not get less or keep shifting from one object to another it is again worth seeking advice. You might discuss with your social worker whether a child guidance clinic could help.

Talking about these difficulties should not blind us to the fact that the vast majority of young foster children will respond in time to those who care for them. Along with all the problems, upsets or naughtiness, these children want to manage, to grow, to love and be loved. As Winnicott put it: 'Each baby is a going concern. In each baby is a vital spark and this urge to development is a part of the baby. . . .' A foster child is also a going concern. It does not all depend on you.

Some useful books

J. Bowlby, *Child Care and the Growth of Love*, Penguin, 1970.
(This book has much influenced child care in Great Britain.)
M. Rutter, *Maternal Deprivation Reassessed*, Penguin, 1972.
(Another look at the same subject—'solid' reading.)
J. and J. Robertson, *Young Children in Brief Separation: a Fresh Look*, Hogarth Press, 1971.
Films relating to the Robertsons' work:
(1) *Kate* (1967) (two years five months, in foster care 27 days)
(2) *Jane* (1968) (seventeen months, in foster care 10 days)
(3) *John* (1969) (seventeen months, in nursery 9 days)
(4) *Thomas* (1971) (two years four months, in foster care 10 days)
(5) *Lucy* (1973) (twenty-one months, in foster care 19 days)
(Any or all of these films are a 'must' for foster parents of young children! Get your social services to organise it.)
J. and E. Wilkes, *Bernard: Bringing Up Our Mongol Son*, Routledge & Kegan Paul, 1974.
(A personal account by parents of their task.)
S. Kerr, *Handicap and Family Crisis*, Pitman, 1975.
(Especially good about problems for the rest of the family.)

H. Jolly, *Book of Child Care: the Complete Guide for Today's Parents*, Allen & Unwin, 1975, is also useful on handicap.

C. Hannam, *Parents and Mentally Handicapped Children*, Penguin, 1975.

4 Parents

Many foster parents are in touch with the parents of children they care for; looking after someone else's child is a very delicate matter and rouses much feeling on both sides. There may be situations in which children are better off without parental contact. This will be discussed later. However, whether or not children see their parents, the attitude of foster parents to their natural parents is important for their psychological well-being. If they see their parents, children need to be able to share the impact of that experience with foster parents. Even young children will pick up 'atmosphere' on such occasions. We know that some children, as they grow older, need urgently to find out about their real parents if contact has been lost — a fact which has recently been acknowledged in the Children Act 1975, which makes it possible for adopted children in England and Wales to find out who their natural parents are. However parents may appear to outsiders, a child has to make his peace with the reality if he is to grow into a mature, well-adjusted person. He is more likely to do so if those who care for him in foster homes or residential care seek to understand his parents because, directly or indirectly, they will communicate that understanding to him. This chapter, therefore, is intended to help foster parents in their attitudes to parents, for the child's sake, the parents' sake and for their own, because this may be one of the hardest aspects of a fostering career.

It is often not easy for foster parents to understand the parents' point of view, for the following reasons.

When people are in difficult situations — as when other people are caring for their children — their feelings are sometimes so painful that they try to conceal them from other people and even from themselves. This makes it hard to help them. Sometimes they show their feelings indirectly in ways which can be very upsetting or irritating to others.

People have very different beliefs about what is the right way to bring up their children but parents are always inclined to think that their beliefs are the sensible and important ones and that other people's are peculiar and wrong-headed!

Although parents of children away from home have the same basic feelings as anyone else, there are a group of these parents (not by any means all) whose behaviour and way of life are very different from those of ordinary foster parents.

When foster parents are caring for someone else's child they often become so fond of the child and concerned about him that it is hard for them to look at the parents objectively, especially if the parents cause distress of any kind to the child.

In this chapter I will write about the first three of these difficulties in understanding parents. The fourth concerns foster parents and is dealt with in the next chapter.

Parents' feelings

Here is part of an actual interview that a social worker, Miss M., had with 'Mrs Campbell', mother of a child in care. The social worker was used to recording very fully and she made sure she wrote it down, immediately

afterwards. Of course it is not word for word accurate but
it is near enough to give you some idea about Mrs
Campbell's fears and feelings about visiting her son,
Alan. Alan was in a children's home but Mrs Campbell's
feelings would have been no different had he been in a
foster home.

Miss M. visited, hoping to persuade Mrs Campbell to
visit Alan, who badly wanted to see her. Mrs Campbell
was in a bad temper and the following conversation took
place.*

Mrs C.	'I'm fed up. He [her husband] keeps me short, spends it all on horses. I've got no more coal after this, anyway, until I get my Family Allowance. I'm sick to death of it. I nearly went last Sunday. I don't care — they can all be put away.'
Miss M.	'You're feeling pretty bad?'
Mrs C.	'I'm feeling bloody awful. I hate this house. I hate him. I hate everybody. He'll be sorry if I go. It will serve him right. I'll show him. I'll give him something to grumble about. He's always grumbling. I'll go and that will give him something to talk about. The lads won't care — they always want him and they don't want me. They can get on with it.'
Miss M.	'I think you hate people more than they hate you. Alan was worried because you hadn't visited.'
Mrs C.	'I'm not visiting him. What good would that do? You took him away from me at that Court, you can get on with it. I'm not going

* I am indebted to a former children's officer for permission to use this
interview.

to see him if he doesn't want me. He doesn't think much of me. He never shows it and I get fed up. I wish he'd show it a bit more if he really does want to see me. Anyway, you took him away and you can go and visit him. Perhaps he'll make a fuss of you.'

Miss M.   'He's awfully like you and you find it difficult to make a fuss of people even when you like them.'

Mrs C.   'No, I'm not going, so don't try to make me. I'm no good to him, anyway, I can't take him things.'

Miss M.   'Giving things doesn't matter much if you go and see him.'

Mrs C.   'You don't understand how I feel. I feel awful when I go there. I know you think I'm hard, but I just can't go. I'm afraid he'll say something he's always saying that he likes his father better than me and I don't see why — I've always done all I can, but it didn't seem to make any difference. He was a terrible baby, always crying. Sometimes I couldn't stop him crying and I felt as though I'd do something dreadful.'

Miss M.   'Yes, you did have a bad time, didn't you?'

Mrs C.   'Bad time? Nobody knows what I had to put up with. Nobody cared — nobody at all. Nobody cares now. I've never had anyone to help me — I never had a soft time when I was a child. My mother used me to do the house-work. I used to have to get up early and do all the housework and my brother didn't do anything. I don't see why I should be expected to do everything for Alan. I bet you think I'm awful.'

Miss M.   'You are painting an awfully black picture of yourself. You have been under a lot of pressure. It hasn't been easy for you.'

Mrs C.   'I suppose I haven't got much excuse really. I used to think I wouldn't get married because my mother and father used to row so much. Then I met him and married him. He seemed all right when I married him. I can't stand him now. He doesn't even keep himself clean and he is awful. Alan came straight away. I used to look at him sometimes and think he might die. He was ever such a little baby. He could have died. He didn't know I was thinking that about him.'

Miss M.   'Alan is very fond of you. He told me how you used to read him stories when he was little. He liked that and he remembered it.'

Mrs C.   'He got better as he got older; somehow he wasn't so bad. I used to wallop him sometimes — I suppose he has told you.'

Miss M.   'No, he talks about the good times at home — those are the ones he remembers.'

Mrs C.   'It's funny he remembers good things — what does he say?'

Miss M.   'Oh, he told me about going to the woods with you in the summer and going to the pictures.'

Mrs C.   'Fancy him remembering that. But I'm fed up with everything. I shall go and leave the lot. . . . Fancy Alan remembering about picnics and that. (Pause.) Want a cup of tea?'

Miss M.   'Yes, please.' (Mrs C. to kitchen to make tea. Returns in a few minutes.)

Mrs C.   'I'm not going to see him, not if you went on your bended knees.'

Miss M.   'Pity, he'll be disappointed.'

Mrs C.   'No, I can't go, it's too difficult.'

Miss M.   'How is it difficult?'

Mrs C.   'Well, the buses don't fit in. Anyway, I can't take him anything.'

Miss M.   'I think you are afraid of the feelings it might stir up.'

Mrs C.   'What? His feelings? He doesn't care.'

Miss M.   'No, your feelings. You probably feel mixed up about him, and I think you have a job to see yourself as anything good.'

Mrs C.   'Well, I'm not much good to him. I had an awful time when he was born. They thought I would die, but I didn't. He was ever such a little baby.'

Miss M.   'You must have been very frightened. It was rather horrid for you.'

Mrs C.   'Yes, they didn't understand how I felt.'

Miss M.   'You have told me a lot of things which you think are bad about you. Alan told me the good side, so I know there are two sides.'

Mrs C.   'Yes, it was funny that he told you he had a nice time at home.'

Miss M.   'You don't appear to the children as a bad mother.'

Mrs C.   'Ah, yes, but what about other people? What about you?'

Miss M.   'Most people are a mixture of good and bad.'

Mrs C.   'I suppose I could get a bus to W — — — on

	Saturday. I wouldn't stay long of course. I don't suppose Alan will be worried. He doesn't really care whether I come or not.'
Miss M.	'Yes he does ask when you are coming.'
Mrs C.	'Oh, that's just because he wants someone to visit him. Anyone would do.'
Miss M.	'That's not true, is it? If it were he would be content just to see me and he isn't. It's you he wants to see.'
Mrs C.	'Well, I don't know. I might go, but it all depends on the buses. Is there one?'
Miss M.	'Yes, there is one you could catch.'
Mrs C.	'I shall go on Saturday to see him. If he wants to see me, of course.'
Miss M.	'Yes, he does.'
Mrs C.	'I'll ring up to say I'm coming.'

We learn many things about Mrs Campbell in this interview — about her childhood, about the difficult times she had with Alan when he was a baby and how frightened she was. But let us concentrate on this question of visiting Alan. She is afraid she is no good as a mother — the fact that Alan had been taken away from home by the Court made this all the worse. She is afraid that Alan will not really want to see her — that he might prefer to see his Dad. She is afraid to go if she cannot take him anything, like sweets, because she feels she has not got enough inside herself to give him as a mother. At first she just says flatly she will not visit, then she makes excuses — the buses don't fit and so on. By the end she says, 'I shall go on Saturday. . . . I'll ring up.' Why does she change her mind? Partly because of the way the social worker is able to show her that Alan remembers good things about her as a mother and gradually a little

F

confidence in herself is restored. Is there anyone who, hearing Mrs Campbell talk like that, would not feel sympathy for her? Yet if she had not been helped to talk about these feelings we might have been left with the impression of a hard, uncaring mother who said: 'You took him from me at that Court — you can get on with it.' If her belligerent attitude at the beginning had called out an angry response in the other person, if what she was saying had been taken at its face value, Alan would not have been visited. This is one of the very important tasks which a social worker has to do, to help parents with deep and complicated feelings about 'failing' their children. It should not ordinarily fall to the lot of the foster parent to have this kind of conversation for they have a different part to play, but it will help foster parents enormously if they can try and understand why the 'Mrs Campbells' sometimes fail to visit or arrive with far too many sweets.

Mrs Campbell has special difficulties and problems, more than ordinary parents. But every one of us has to find ways of hiding from ourselves and other people feelings that are too sore. It would be easy to sympathise if parents came and said: 'I feel so awful about Johnny.' But it is not like that. They try to cover it up.

One way of covering up is to try to blame someone else entirely for what has gone wrong. We all do it. For example, it was 'his fault' or 'his mother's fault' that her marriage went wrong and the family broke up. In this way, parents may hide from themselves and from other people their guilt. It is not possible to force anyone into accepting some of the responsibility for their troubles. Mrs Campbell began by blaming things on her husband but with sympathy came to talk about her feelings that she had failed as a mother. Occasionally, we see this tendency to blame others developed to an abnormal degree when it becomes a form of mental illness. Such unfortunate people see 'the whole world against them', or certain people trying to 'do them down' at every turn. But this is only an extreme version of a way we all have of looking for outside causes to explain away our troubles to ourselves.

Some parents try to manage uncomfortable feelings about failing their children by finding fault with the care the foster parents give. This is extremely common and is responsible for a lot of the friction that occurs between foster parents and parents. This arises even when children are away from home for short periods and for reasons which reflect no discredit on the parents. It often crops up over something quite trivial — like clothing. For example, foster parents may return a child home with clothes all carefully laundered and perhaps some new ones too. The next thing is that the parents say he hasn't got his blue trousers. Perhaps the trousers were too small when he came and split the first time he wore them so you threw them out. Or perhaps you are sure you had returned them. This kind of incident rouses very strong feelings in foster parents who are quite naturally touchy about their care of the child and his clothing. But it may be difficult, if not impossible, for parents to bear that someone may have looked after their child better than they do and the way out of this for them is to find something to criticise. Incidentally, I am not suggesting that foster parents never slip up; his blue trousers may have been forgotten — but if you know you did not and if you find this kind of incident cropping up often, it may be helpful to ask yourself what lies behind the criticism; this may make it easier to bear.

Another thing we all do is to run away from the object of our guilt, to try and forget about it. It is very hard to understand this when we speak of parents and children, though it is easy enough to recognise in more trivial things — like avoiding someone in the street whom we feel guilty about for some reason or another. The ties of parent and child are normally so close that to try and 'forget' your child seems unnatural to ordinary parents. Nevertheless, we do find that for some, like Mrs Campbell, this is the way they try to avoid painful feelings. It may take the form of actually physically running away, as when mothers move to another area and leave no address, or it may be more like emotionally running away, as when visits are at the last moment funked and the child is left disappointed and hurt. This last is terribly hard for foster parents to bear.

Some parents try and 'make up' to the child in ways that are exaggerated and unhelpful. Into this category come foolishly expensive presents which foster parents may feel are not really valued by the child and which they, the foster parents, cannot afford to give him themselves. Then there are wild promises to the child: 'I'm getting a flat and I'll have you home soon' — when it's no way certain; or 'I've got a new job and I'll buy you a bicycle' — when the bicycle never comes . . . and so on.

Thus in all kinds of ways parents try to hide from their guilty feelings or to find rather clumsy ways of putting things right, making a kind of assertion that they are still the important person in their children's lives. Of course, if they could face their guilt and try to sort out their muddled feelings about their children, this would be best. But this is very difficult for any one of us, and sometimes it is too much for people like Mrs Campbell to bear, especially when it is success and failure as parents which is at stake. The more we know of the struggles and suffering of some parents from childhood onwards, the harder it becomes to judge and condemn them for their failures.

Other ways of bringing up children

People in other parts of the world have ways of bringing up their children which are totally different from our own. The ages at which children are weaned from the breast, or toilet trained, for example, vary greatly in different parts of the world, as do the ways in which mothers carry out the weaning or toilet training. This is not simply that parents do different things; it is that parents believe in different methods of bringing up children and have different ideas about what they want to achieve.

Some of you who read this book will have had the experience of fostering children whose parents are not British and you may have come across some quite dramatic examples of ways in which parents' ideas and methods differed from your own. Sometimes we need to go back to the way of life in the person's home country before we can begin to understand their attitudes toward their children.

Take, for example, West Indian parents who have come in such numbers to this country. Long ago, in the West Indies, slaves were not allowed to marry; for this reason, legal marriage is not taken for granted amongst West Indians as it is by most people in our country and West Indians do not worry so much about children being illegitimate. Added to this, the West Indian 'family' is a much wider affair than ours with all sorts of relations playing a part in the bringing up of children. Therefore the illegitimate child and his mother were not lonely and isolated as they so often are in our country. West Indian mothers who came to this country have been bewildered to find that there is a stigma on them for being unmarried and that it is much harder for them over here to bring up their children without a husband. They have been traditionally used to letting a number of people share in the care of their children and may not feel at all guilty about asking for their children to be placed in foster homes — in contrast to the majority of British mothers.

We need not go to other countries, however, to find these important differences in attitudes and beliefs about child rearing. Even within our own country and within one town there are striking contrasts between different groups of parents. For instance, John and Elizabeth Newson,* psychologists at Nottingham University, have interviewed over 700 mothers when their children were at different ages and their findings show clearly many differences between the mothers of Nottingham. For example, there is a great deal of difference between mothers about letting babies have things to suck, once they are on solid food. One group of mothers was very worried if the child continued to want a bottle 'for comfort' after the usual stage of weaning and would do their best to break him of it. Another group of mothers did not mind about this at all and their children had comforters of one sort or another for as long as they wanted. Similarly, there were big differences between groups of mothers in their attitudes to little children playing with their genitals; some were much more concerned than others to stop it.

In the examples above the difference between groups of mothers were connected with class. It was the middle-class mothers who worried most about continued

* See p. 33.

sucking; it was the working-class mothers who worried most about children playing with their genitals.

But of course it is not only social class that distinguishes groups of people—studies in different parts of the country might reveal some fascinating differences in ways of bringing up children, even between roughly the same social classes.

These are only a few examples of a huge subject. There are two vital things to remember. First, your foster child has, for months or years, been getting accustomed to an upbringing which may differ greatly from the one you gave your own children. It will not get you very far to think which is 'the right way' or 'the wrong way'. To help the child most, you need to learn something about his parents' beliefs and methods of child rearing so that you can bridge the gap and not increase the shock of his separation by handling the child in very different ways and having quite different expectations of him. For example, if a three-year-old comes sucking his bottle, you will go easy and let him keep what he is used to; if a baby has clearly been accustomed to a great deal of attention and very little time on his own, you will not leave him in the garden in his pram for long at first, though you might have done this quite happily with your own. You may find your foster child has been used to going to bed at very different times from your own children. For your convenience, he may have to do things your way but it will help you to handle the situation sensitively if you know what he has been used to. Some of this can be judged simply by observing the foster child; other things will be puzzling till more is known about the home he has come from.

Second, your attitude to the parents themselves (and therefore indirectly the child) will be more tolerant the more you learn about these differences between groups of parents as well as between individual people. It gives us a healthy jolt to be made to think, 'Why do I consider that so and so is important?' when it is obvious someone else does not — or vice versa. Such knowledge makes us less dogmatic in our attitudes: it will also make the job of fostering more interesting.

The special problems of some parents
Even within one group, whether it is 'the West Indians' or 'the middle classes' or whatever, there will be some parents with particular personality difficulties. Although quite a number of parents of children away from home will be just ordinary people with an ordinary share of human problems and human weaknesses, there are a proportion who have serious psychological problems which the foster parents may never have encountered until they took on foster children. You may never have known anyone before who was seriously ill mentally; or a mother who neglects her children, for example. It is a job for the expert to study the causes of these problems about which we know far too little at present but there are certain lines of thought about such parents which may be helpful to foster parents.

We can divide parents of children away from home into three very broad categories, excluding those who are simply in temporary difficulty about caring for their children and who have no long-term problems; an example of this would be mothers expecting new babies who have moved away from friends and relatives to a new housing estate, though, as I suggested earlier, even such straightforward situations often have some complication — e.g., a quarrel with grandmother who might have looked after the child.

(1) Those who have a recognised form of mental illness or who are mentally handicapped.

(2) Those who, although not called 'mentally ill', have all kinds of major problems in their family life and whose behaviour is clearly unusual by comparison with others. For example, where children are neglected, or there are very low standards in the home.

(3) Lone parents — that is, where there is only one parent in the home, whether through illegitimacy, divorce, separation, or death.

Of course, these categories may overlap — the mother of an illegitimate child may be mentally ill or subnormal, for example. But for clarity's sake, it is easier to discuss the special problems of these groups one by one.

Most readers will know that there is a distinction between 'mentally ill' and the 'mentally handicapped'. This is not a hard and fast division, for it is quite possible for people to suffer from both kinds of disability. For practical purposes, however, they can be separated. The phrase 'mental handicap' implies that the person is not as intelligent as the average person in our society; mental illness is not necessarily related to high or low intelligence; it is, as the name suggests, a severe disturbance of feeling and behaviour.

Mental illness

Mental illnesses are sometimes divided into two kinds, the 'psychotic' and the 'neurotic' illnesses, though the divisions are not always clear-cut. We cannot say that the one is more serious than the other for, to the people concerned, both are deeply distressing and both can be either sudden or gradual, short-lived or long-drawn-out. The psychotic illness is the kind which we normally associate with the word 'madness', for such people do seem odder and less in touch with the real world than the neurotic person and this is why such illnesses may be more frightening to us. In this connection, we do well to remember that only a very small proportion of mentally ill people ever become violent and nowadays modern drug treatment has made this a rare occurrence.

The policy in recent years has been to keep people in mental hospitals for as short a time as possible and to let them live ordinary lives at home, wherever it is practicable. It has been found that some mentally ill people actually got worse in the hospital environment, or did not recover as quickly as they might have done. This was partly because of the way hospitals used to be run and more has been done now to improve the life of the patient in all kinds of ways — to give him more stimulus, more outside interests and so on. But even so, hospital is hospital; and doctors are keen that anyone who can manage out of hospital should do so.

Our attitudes to mental illness have changed a great deal in recent years and we no longer see the problem in 'they and us' terms. That is to say, we understand that most of us are a 'little bit ill' at times; we have days when we are depressed for no particular reason; days when we are fussy and anxious beyond what the situation calls for; days when we cannot seem to feel much about anybody, even the nearest and dearest. All these feelings and many others are seen in more striking and dramatic forms in mental illness. Whether or not help is called for will often depend to quite an extent on the family and friends; some mentally ill people never call in the doctor because they are so well supported that they are 'tided over' until such time as recovery comes about naturally.

Most people find it easier to understand the feelings of

people suffering from neurotic rather than psychotic illness, though this will not always be so. Feeling guilty, depressed, anxious and so on, which is a part of neurotic illness, is also a part of everyday life. In any case there will be some who read this book who have experienced some form of mental illness. They will know that the descriptions which follow are shallow, for no words of mine can recreate the deep, painful feelings which they have experienced. To them I apologise. Their 'inside knowledge' may prove of great help in their relationship with others who are mentally ill, provided they can stand apart from their past suffering and are not still too involved in it.

Mentally ill parents of young children will often be 'out and about', sometimes after quite a short spell in hospital, having treatment perhaps at outpatient clinics or drugs from their general practitioner. They will want to visit their children and in most cases it will be natural and right for them to do so. Of course there will be occasions when this contact will not be desirable. It may be that the child has no hope of ever returning and that the illness is too frightening or too distressing to him; or that the parent for a time cannot face visiting; or that the foster parents feel they cannot cope with it. There are endless possible complications in this kind of situation and it is part of the social worker's task to try and help sort out the feelings of everyone concerned in it. The social worker may also help by supporting foster parents and the parents in such visits — for example by bringing the parent to the foster home.

Mental illnesses, like physical illnesses, are of different kinds. However, they are not easy to put into separate compartments and psychiatrists themselves will admit that some of these tidy categories are only tidy in theory — in practice they overlap. I am not going to describe all these categories — simply to comment on three kinds of illness which foster parents might encounter. Nor am I going to discuss causes and treatment of mental illness for there are many differences of opinion between experts and much remains to be discovered.

Schizophrenia   This is one of the psychotic illnesses. The word means 'split mind' but not in the sense of the person being 'two different people', like Jekyll and Hyde. The split is between the world outside and the world inside. The schizophrenic cannot feel himself to be a real person in a real world; he feels in some way different and apart and cannot communicate. Someone has said there seems to be a 'wall of glass' between you and the schizophrenic. This is one of the most serious illnesses in the sense that it can, over a period of years, so alter the personality that the person becomes unable to form normal relationships. However, it must be emphasised that this is not always the case. There are a number of examples of people who have recovered from this illness and led ordinary lives afterwards. Modern drugs and other treatments can control acute phases and help patients back into ordinary life, though there is no cure at the present time,

There are many different ways in which this illness shows itself. It may be that the person seems to be in a world of his own unconnected with yours, and you may feel that you cannot get near to him, or that he is following trains of thought which you cannot understand. Sometimes there is a certain 'flatness' in the way such a person responds, as if they felt almost dead inside. All this is a part of the illness and once you understand that you will be less frightened by it. You will also realise that such illnesses may make it impossible for a parent to respond appropriately to their children; for example, a schizophrenic mother might be unable to show warmth and affection to the child, even if the child seemed to be asking for it. Some of such people are the most 'odd' you are likely to meet; they will immediately strike you as strange in a way other mentally ill people do not.

Depression   We all have phases of 'feeling depressed' but for some people the feelings become so acute that treatment is necessary. A very large proportion of people admitted to mental hospitals are suffering from depression. Nowadays the majority of people who go to hospital suffering from depression are there for only a few weeks and respond quite quickly to various forms of treatment. Treatment seems to cut short the natural course of the illness. The feelings of hopelessness, of apathy, of the world being utterly black are familiar in some degree to everyone so that the depressed person is no stranger to us, as the schizophrenic may be. But instead of helping us to be more sympathetic this can work the opposite way. For we may say in effect: 'I have felt miserable and got over it — why can't this person buck up and make an effort?' Indeed, it is quite common for depressed people to be told to 'cheer up'. It is quite impossible for a person who is seriously depressed to 'snap out of it' and the fact that we manage to overcome these feelings in ourselves is absolutely no indication that they can do the same. Quite a number of children come into care because their mothers are suffering from depression of this kind. Foster parents may have quite a lot to do with them when they are out of hospital but not yet well enough to have the children home. It is important to remember at this stage that, although you can help by supporting and encouraging the mother in the efforts she makes, you cannot force the pace by the 'pull your socks up' method. One of the feelings associated with this illness is excessive guilt about many things and such people frequently reproach themselves for failing as wives or husbands or as parents. It is important not to increase this guilt by any kind of implied or open criticism, even if in fact they have failed in some respects. On the other hand, once you have a good relationship with such a mother, praise for what has been done well can be a spur if the mother has started on the road to recovery — it does not help when the illness is at its most acute. Being depressed is like having shoes made of lead — everything is an effort, even trivial things like finding out the times of the buses to visit the children. If you understand this you will be able to accept the failures more easily and value the efforts that the person does make.

There is another symptom sometimes associated with depression — that of anxiety. The person does not simply feel 'empty' and miserable but gets agitated as well and very worked up about things that seem trivial to others. Here again, it is not helpful to try and argue anyone out of it; it can help, however, when people are not too ill to share the burden of their anxiety in practical ways. Such a mother, for example, might find the anxiety of deciding what to buy for her child's birthday too great and would welcome your help.

Rituals and routines   We all have routines; life would be much more effort if we did not have them because they enable us to do certain things regularly without thinking about them. Most of us get a kind of comfort and enjoyment out of doing familiar things especially at times of stress, when the oft-repeated actions seem somehow reassuring—like making a cup of tea or feeding the cat. There is, however, a kind of mental illness in which people, because of some deep inner anxieties, become too dependent on these routines and rituals and have to invent more and more elaborate ones to try somehow to keep the anxiety at bay. This is very painful for them because one bit of them is quite able to see that it is silly; yet they cannot help it. Such people have many different kinds of 'ritual' but it is often related to cleanliness and amongst housewives it may take the form of a great preoccupation with cleaning the house and with complicated routines about the time and the way the cleaning is done. This sometimes results in neglect of other duties—like cooking or time to play with the children. It can dominate the person's mind so much that the whole family somehow gets drawn into the problem, especially where something like house-cleaning is involved, for husbands and children may not be allowed to make an ordinary amount of mess.

As with all the other forms of illness, the vital thing to grasp is that this is really beyond the person's control and that they often despise themselves for needing to have these routines and rituals. With treatment some people can be helped to keep them from spreading into everything. Thus they can live a reasonably ordinary life.

The most valuable thing that foster parents can do for any parents who are mentally ill is to try and grasp what it feels like to them, the confusion, the anxiety, the despair they may be feeling and try and behave towards them as ordinary people with problems like themselves—only more so. But there will be some forms of mental illness you will find harder to bear than others. This is natural and inevitable; it is partly because of your own particular temperament; partly because some illnesses bring out less pleasant characteristics in the person. For example, if a person is exceedingly tense and anxious, he is more prone to bursts of irritability or anger than if he is well.

What of the young child and his mentally ill parent? How long he has been with a mentally ill parent and who else has been caring for him will affect the degree to which he has been disturbed by it. But we cannot say with any certainty in any particular case what his reaction will be, for children's responses are infinitely varied. It is clear, however, that in the close intimate tie between the child and his parents, especially the mother, even very young children will be in some way aware of their mother's state of mind and react to it.

> Baby Mark's mother gradually became more and more depressed in the first year of his life. As the months went by and she became iller, this little boy became more and more cheerful and active. At first everybody thought he was just a bonny happy boy; but gradually it was seen that he was too active, ceaselessly laughing and grimacing and on the move. It seemed as if he was trying to cheer his mother up or to be the 'live' one in the partnership.

When you receive a child into your home, from the care of a mentally ill parent, try and see how he has reacted to it; sometimes there will be little to show you; sometimes it will seem as if the child—even quite a young one—has had to be too grown up, in an attempt to help the parent; this can be so even with very young children, as the following example shows:

> Kathleen M. was three: her mother was seriously depressed and lay in bed for long spells of the day, unable to get up. Kathleen, an intelligent bright little girl, had become very protective of her mother, trying

to look after her. When the social worker visited the home Mrs M. would not get up to unlock the door, Kathleen, who could not manage the lock, said — 'Be a good girl, Mummy, open the door for Miss W. there's a good girl'. . . . Kathleen eventually had to leave home and was fostered. Her great need was to be an ordinary little girl again but for several weeks she was greatly worried — 'Who was looking after Mummy?' The foster mother's task was to help her to be a little girl again, though it might be necessary for a time to find an outlet for Kathleen's protectiveness — for example, in the care of an animal or bird.

Sometimes the child has imitated the behaviour of the parent and foster parents fear that he may himself be mentally disturbed — only to find that once he is away from the parent, he quickly recovers. At other times he will have been more deeply affected by his contact with mental illness. Some readers may have heard of children who are severely mentally ill or 'psychotic'. These are very few in number and the reasons for this are as yet obscure and controversial. There is absolutely no reason to assume that a young child coming from the care of a mentally ill parent will be himself mentally ill in the sense of having a recognised form of illness — that is highly improbable. He may of course be deeply distressed emotionally and in that sense could be called 'ill' but that is not the same as the rare and tragic case of the 'psychotic' child.

Mental handicap
People who are severely subnormal do not usually have children since they are undeveloped physically as well as

G

mentally. But there is a group of girls who are, as we might put it, 'a bit simple' — clearly below the average in intelligence — and who are particularly likely to get into difficulties of one kind and another. Whether they do or not depends partly on their family backgrounds, and the kind of support and control which they get. Many such girls live fairly normal lives and make quite stable, successful marriages — especially if the man they marry is of higher intelligence and enjoys taking charge of the situation. But some of these girls of this kind have illegitimate babies and are emotionally disturbed in addition to being of limited intelligence. Quite often they are themselves deprived children from broken or unstable homes.

The following example shows how a foster home can play a vital part in helping such a girl settle down as well as giving excellent care to her baby.

Miss Croft was twenty-eight. She had been in a children's home till she was fourteen; was of low intelligence and thought to be unfit at fourteen to go out to work. She had therefore been sent to a mental deficiency institution — as they were then called. She was sent out 'on trial' to domestic jobs but was recalled three times because she became pregnant. She had Anthony, Peter and Gloria, and the two boys were taken from her a few weeks after birth, for it seemed she would not be able to care for them by herself; Anthony went into a residential nursery and then to children's homes; Peter went to a permanent foster home. Miss Croft was not encouraged to keep in touch with her sons although she had looked after them beautifully as babies in the first few weeks and showed much emotion about parting from them. She actually said: 'if you take Peter away from me, I'll have another one', but was too limited in intelligence and lacking in confidence to insist on seeing them.

A different plan was made after Gloria was born. Foster parents were found with older children of their own, who accepted Miss Croft as a welcome visitor to their home. She came regularly to the foster home, stayed overnight sometimes, put Gloria to bed, knitted for her and so on. Gloria flourished — she was a beautiful, active red-headed little girl of whom any mother could be proud. Miss Croft went out 'on trial' from the hospital again and this time completed the necessary period of time successfully. She did not become pregnant while out of the hospital. A year or two later she married and had a child; and she later gave willing consent to Gloria's adoption.

Miss Croft has been 'a deprived child' — she never felt she had anything of her own to belong to and to love; she protested in the only way she could against the loss of her babies — by having another one. But this only led to further loss of liberty and so the vicious circle went on repeating itself until she was allowed to play a part in Gloria's upbringing and made to feel a welcome guest in the foster home. In this way, she was somehow freed to move into a more stable and settled life.

Foster parents who have contact with such girls will often feel protective and sympathetic towards them, for they are in many ways so like children themselves. The story of Miss Croft began in the days when the care of the deprived, not very intelligent child was far less understanding than it is now. Policies regarding the care of the mentally handicapped have changed a great deal; girls are no longer kept in institutions for any longer than is absolutely necessary and, as with the mentally ill, they are encouraged to live ordinary lives. But nevertheless, foster parents may have an important role in helping them stabilise and grow up; they are often late developers emotionally and can make quite successful marriages later on in their lives.

Inadequate parents
The word 'inadequate' is rather vague. After all, people who are mentally ill or subnormal may be in some ways 'inadequate parents'. But there are a group of parents who do not fall clearly into either of those two categories, although it is obvious that they have difficulty in behaving like ordinary parents and in caring for their children in ways we think desirable. These may be the parents who neglect or ill-treat their children, or whose homes are of a very low standard, who are in serious debt, whose marriages are very unstable, whose way of life we might consider immoral, and so on. One may find some or all of these problems in one family; they may be linked with low intelligence or recognised mental illness or they may not. Various words are applied to parents like this — sometimes they are called 'immature', sometimes we refer to 'problem families'. But there is a danger in this kind of label. They may be used without real understanding, or with a kind of implied superiority, or to avoid really trying to understand how such parents feel. So let us leave the labels aside and think about the people as sensitively as we can.

We know that childhood experiences are very important in shaping future development; we have to remind ourselves that the parents were children once. We find over and over again with tragic regularity that where parents reject, neglect or ill-treat their children they were themselves rejected, neglected or ill-treated. We had, in Mrs Campbell at the beginning of this chapter, an example of a mother whose anger and resentment seemed to go back to her own childhood when she felt 'nobody cared'. Now it is obvious that not all unhappy children make unsuccessful parents; some people reading this book may have had a bad time when they were children and yet have reared their own children without undue difficulty. Clearly, there is a great deal we do not yet understand about this; it may well be that some are endowed with inner strengths which enable them to grow up healthily in their feelings as well as their bodies, despite experiences which stunt the growth of others. Or it may be that if there is something warm and good at some time between a child and someone—his parent or parent substitutes—this gives him a solid core and enables him to stand the suffering. We are still uncertain why some manage to overcome the past and some do not. But the more we get to know about other people's backgrounds, the more certain we become that it is useless to sit in judgment, for we simply do not know and can never know whether someone could or could not have behaved differently, could or could not have overcome their childhood suffering, as some of you may have done. Some parents are stuck and they cannot give to their children what they themselves have never had. They are child-like. Now all of us have inside us the child we once were—and from time to time it shows and we behave in a childish way. But for these people, this childish behaviour is their dominant characteristic. They are not grown up for most of the time. Ways of behaving that are normal to the little child at two, three or four years old persist into adult life. Thus it is normal for the small child to be bad at waiting for things; for him to want the pretty things in

front of him today rather than the sensible thing
tomorrow. It is normal for his moods to change very
quickly and for him to have temper-tantrums. These
things and many more you accept without question in the
small child. But when we see them in adults, we are
surprised and shocked. The parent who cannot resist
buying an expensive walkie-talkie doll at the door when
the children need clothes desperately; the parent who has
sudden outbursts of violent temper and strikes a child;
the parent who like the ordinary little child cannot hold
the memory and the image of other people in his mind for
long and so seems to forget his children; this is strange
indeed in the adult. It is much harder to feel sympathetic
towards such people than towards those who are quite
obviously mentally ill; yet they need our compassion and
understanding just as much.

Cruel or neglectful parents
Of all the problems which such parents may show, it is
cruelty and neglect of children which is the most painful
for foster parents to think about and the most difficult to
understand. Nothing can or should ever remove the shock
and pain we all feel about such actions because it is
natural and wholesome to react like that. Yet if foster
parents are to meet such parents they have to go on from
the first sense of outrage to a more constructive attempt
to understand the problem. As I said earlier, neither
serious neglect nor cruelty to children are at all common.
Yet it happens.

Why do parents neglect their children? There are a
host of reasons. Sometimes it is sheer physical and
emotional exhaustion: for example, when a not very
intelligent woman has too many children in quick
succession and it all gets beyond her; although there are

usually complicating factors such as bad housing, poor food and so on. Sometimes if the marriage is in danger of going on the rocks, the mother may be so frantic about it that she somehow has no energy to spare for her children.

Sometimes the reason lies deep in the person because of their own deprivation in childhood. They feel empty themselves and fear that they have nothing to give — like Mrs Campbell at the beginning of this chapter.

What of cruelty? There are many different kinds of cruelty of which physical ill-treatment is only one. There are other more subtle forms of mental cruelty also damaging to the child. How can people do such things? All parents have mixed feelings about their children — love mixed with anger and even resentment at times — but love usually triumphs. You will recall that earlier in this book I described the mixed feelings about parents which children have; most of us do not have too much difficulty about seeing these. But it is much harder to admit to the reverse — that parents have mixed feelings about their children. There is a bit of a conspiracy to deny this; for example, when a woman is expecting a baby, it is generally assumed she ought to be delighted. Yet if we are honest we know that there are times when she is not, when she is resentful and annoyed and wishes it had never happened. Then there are moments when an ordinary parent experiences a suddenly irrational blaze of anger towards his child and hastily — and guiltily — pushes it away and regains control. Thus we have to allow that cruel parents are not utterly and completely different from ourselves but, in their mixture of feelings, the angry, resentful feelings have somehow got the upper hand. This is terrifying to every one of us and may provoke violent reactions against them. Cruelty is ugly; but the people who are cruel suffer as well, for they are in a private hell, which we can only guess at.

We know now something of the experiences and characteristics of parents who ill-treat their children physically. In a high proportion of cases, one or both of the parents (and that may include a step-parent) have been seriously deprived and/or physically ill treated themselves as children. They have often married young. Some years ago, some experiments with monkeys in the USA showed that monkeys who had themselves been deprived in babyhood had much difficulty in establishing normal sexual relationships and, later, in being caring parents. This strongly confirms what many of us have observed in daily experience in the field of child welfare. Similarly, just as every farmer knows how important it is for an animal to establish a bond with the new-born in the first few hours of life, so with humans we now know that early 'bonding', as we call it, is vital. It has been found that a number of mothers who ill-treat their children were separated from them at birth through prematurity or illness.

One of the strangest aspects of this problem is that cruel parents often seem to have expectations of their infant's capacity to control himself (his crying, his bladder, his bowels, etc.) which are quite unrealistic. It is almost as if they were expecting the child to be an adult before his time and they therefore see the relationship as a battle of wills. If a foster parent notices that a parent seems unnaturally upset by behaviour normal for a young child and especially if the parent suggests the child 'did it on purpose to annoy', this is a matter which should be discussed with the social worker.

It is also obvious that being a step-parent may impose some strain on family relationships. We must be very cautious about this: thousands of step-parents manage their new families admirably, despite some awkward moments with resentful children! But, now and again, the step-parent is unable to cope with the intensity of feelings on both sides and there is an explosion.

It has been observed that in many cases of cruelty, it is not easy to establish which parent is responsible, for one protects the other. Nor is it common for there to be callous indifference. Often, the parents rush the child to hospital, explaining there has been an accident.

I stressed earlier that this whole matter has to be kept in proportion. But if cruelty is established, foster parents should bear in mind that total rejection is rare. When that happens, the problem is easier to resolve, for one must seek permanent, substitute care for the child. The problem for the social workers is when there is a powerful mixture of loving and hating feelings in the parents. It has been suggested that in such cases, since the child's welfare is the first consideration, to settle him and keep in a loving adoptive or foster home should be the only duty of the social worker. There will undoubtedly be cases where this is right. But I would ask you to bear in mind that, in reaching such a decision, social workers have to believe that they are justified in taking away a child for ever from his parents, that they (the parents) cannot be helped to control their angry feelings. Some such children will, despite it all, have formed a deep attachment to their parents. Social workers also know, from experience, that a life in care is not always as settled as it may appear at the time. Just as parents fail, so do foster parents when unforeseen and unforeseeable stresses come upon them. Indeed, occasionally foster parents, as parents, physically ill-treat children.

Writing these words, there is always a danger that people will think I am 'on the side' of the parents. That is not so. I believe that every case is unique, and that we can have no hard and fast rules about the best course of action for all young children who have been ill treated. I am sure, however, that the more foster parents can understand the parents' problems, the better for all concerned in the long run. Some legal aspects of the relationship between foster parents and parents are discussed in chapter 5.

One-parent families

We have not made it easy in this country for lone parents to bring up their children. A recent Government Committee* showed in how many ways the single parent has been at a disadvantage, financially, materially, socially and psychologically. There is no doubt, however, that very slowly things are improving. There has been some improvement in social security allowances, some development of nursery school and play group facilities, for working mothers; certainly there is less stigma for those who are unmarried, divorced or separated; generally, the social climate has changed so that it is now possible for a lone parent to make a real choice as to whether to bring the child up or look for substitute care. In the past, the dice were so heavily loaded that in many instances, it could not be said to be a real choice. There is even a greater willingness now to accept a father's right to stay at home and look after his children if he wishes and a social security allowance will be paid to him. (A good many fathers still prefer their children to be cared for by others, however. For instance, in 1972, 5 per cent of the children who came into care did so because of the death or desertion of their mother.) None the less it is less likely

* *Report of the Committee on One Parent Families* (DHSS) (Finer Report), HMSO, 1974.

now than in the past that foster parents will be asked to care for children simply because they come from one-parent families. The probability is that there will be special strains or difficulties which have made the position temporarily or permanently unmanageable. For example, in 1972, less than 2 per cent of children coming into care were said to have come into care *specifically* because they were illegitimate and their mothers were unable to provide for them. Most local authorities would do their best to encourage lone parents to keep their children with various kinds of community support.

That is not to say, however, that many of the thousands of children who come into care, ostensibly because of parental illness, do not come from homes in which there is only one parent. Clearly they do so. Physical and mental illness may be brought about by the strains of a marital breakdown and 'coping' alone and, when it occurs, maybe the very fact of being alone increases the likelihood of having to look for a substitute home for their child. Such parents may look with envy upon the seemingly 'ordinary' family life of the foster parent and you may be surprised if they are, on occasions, 'prickly' when they visit you. You may know of your own worries and anxieties — they do not and it may seem to them the luck is all on your side. If you detect such feelings and they are not too overwhelmed with their own worries, it may sometimes be helpful to them to share some of your troubles, past and present. It's all a matter of timing!

Some mothers of illegitimate babies cannot make up their minds early on to place their child for adoption and yet find it very difficult to allow him to get fond of the foster parents. Such a situation is not uncommon with children placed in private foster homes and is sometimes the reason for their being moved from one foster home to another. This is bound to be bad for the children. Although the legal powers of social service departments are limited, you should seek advice from social workers if you have such a child. It may be possible to help the mother sort out her feelings to prevent these moves.

Where parents of the children are divorced or separated — and indeed even when parents are together but unhappily married — foster parents will often be drawn into hearing the story of the other partner's misdeeds. A word of warning here; it may help parents to talk of these matters, but it is very difficult to avoid taking sides. Yet to do so is not really helpful. Experience has shown that the old saying 'six of one and half a dozen of the other' is never truer than in marriage troubles. It is also very important that you should know what the exact legal position is with regard to access to the children by both parents. If your social worker is unclear you should ask for a solicitor to be consulted. The children may sometimes be used as a pawn and, as foster parents, you may have a painful and difficult task in helping children who may have affection and loyalty to both parents.

This chapter has looked at things mainly from the point of view of parents' feelings and how foster parents can help them. But I do not forget that the foster parents have feelings too and that is what the next chapter is about.

Some useful books

The Newsons' books (see p. 33) are relevant.
B. Maddox, *The Half-Parent*, Deutsch, 1975.
(A personal account of what it's like.)
D. Marsden, *Mothers Alone*, Penguin, 1970
The Maltreated Child, ed. J. Carter, Priory Press, 1974.
(Various aspects of child abuse, objectively discussed.)
R. Mitchell, *Depression*, Penguin, 1975.
J. Emerson and C. Wallace, *Schizophrenia, the Divided Mind*, obtainable from the 'Mind' bookshop.

5 Foster parents

So far this book has been about children and their parents. But foster parents get tired of having other people's feelings and attitudes explained to them for they have a right to their own and they need from time to time to think about themselves in relation to this task of fostering. For the plain fact is that taking a foster child can make a great difference to you and to your family life in all sorts of ways, some enriching, some disturbing.

Before fostering

Apart from the effect which an individual child has on your family, there is the business of being a foster parent in itself. What does this entail? You may take a child for weeks, months or years or you may occasionally make him a permanent member of your family. Not infrequently, it turns out differently from what was expected. Sometimes he comes for a few weeks and stays for years; sometimes he comes for six months and goes home in a week. The first thing to ask yourself therefore is, 'Can we cope with this kind of uncertainty?' For the one certain thing about fostering is uncertainty — about length of stay, about the child's reactions, about his parents, even about the actual time he is going to arrive. It is not uncommon for foster parents to be asked in the morning to take some children in the afternoon; the foster mother rushes round, tidying up and preparing; then at 3.30 p.m. the social worker returns empty-handed to say that Granny at the last moment relented and said she will have the children after all. Now you may be an excellent parent to your own children but find this kind of uncertainty difficult to bear. On the other hand, you may enjoy this kind of situation and relish the excitement and change it brings into your everyday life. Of course that particular illustration applies particularly to those who foster short-stay children, but inherent in all fostering is this element of uncertainty in one form or another.

Another thing to recognise from the start is that most people who foster—even when they make a private arrangement with the parents—will have some kind of contact with local authorities or voluntary organisations.* If you take a child who is in care of the children's department or a voluntary organisation, you enter into a relationship with the people who placed him with you. As I mentioned in chapter 1, the social worker has a statutory responsibility to see that all is well, and every sensible person will see that this is necessary. But her concern goes far beyond simply 'inspecting' the foster home and seeing a child is well treated physically, vitally important though these duties are. The social worker should take an interest in every aspect of a child's well-being—his contact with his parents, how he is developing mentally and emotionally as well as physically and so on. The fact that the foster parents may experience some problems or difficulties does not necessarily imply any reflection on their worth as foster parents, for we have learnt over the years that there are sensitive adjustments to be made on both sides when a child enters a foster home and this may take time. The

* See chapter 1.

social worker is there to help the foster parents wherever possible over these adjustments. You are never completely on your own as foster parents — unlike adoption, where after a preliminary period, the child is in every way as one of your own. Now there are two ways of looking at this. You may see this continuing contact with 'officials' as an intrusion on your family privacy and you may prefer to get on with the job, independently. Or you may be glad to share with someone else some of the inevitable stresses and strains, especially if there is sympathy towards your feelings as well as the child's. You may also enjoy the feeling of belonging to an organisation set up to care for children and of being part of a service of this kind. How you feel will be determined to some extent by your actual experiences with the social worker concerned and obviously, some social workers are better than others, like foster parents — and there will be some whom you take to particularly, others whom you do not. Yet it is not just a question of personalities. It is partly a question of whether or not you like to feel that you are a member of a team. If you prefer to play a lone hand and dislike the idea of what is, inevitably, a kind of 'interference', then you probably would do better not to foster children who will bring you in contact with officialdom.

Let us suppose, however, that you like the element of uncertainty and are quite happy about visits from a social worker: so, undeterred, you apply,* and a social worker comes to see you. It is perfectly natural to feel a bit nervous in this situation — everyone does. After all, offering a home to a child is a big step and no one likes to think that they might be rejected because that might

---

* Applications to foster can be made to the social services department of your local authority; or to such voluntary organisations as those referred to in chapter 1.

seem to imply that they were not suitable people to be parents. What I have described in this book so far about the problems of the children and their parents should have made it abundantly clear that fostering is no longer — if it ever was — simply a question of being a good parent. Therefore not to be accepted does not carry that implication. There may be dozens of reasons, some obvious, like the effect a foster child might have on your own child. A social worker wants to obtain from prospective foster parents as full a picture as possible of their family life in order to see what kinds of children — ages, backgrounds, personalities, etc. might fit in best. She will often want to see them several times and this does not necessarily mean she thinks something is wrong! She wants not only to protect the child but to protect them from the suffering which unsuccessful fostering can cause. That may sound a bit dramatic but if some of those reading this book have had unhappy experiences over fostering they will know how distressing it can be to the foster parents when they find for one reason or another it is too much for them. An equally important reason for a number of visits from the social worker is to enable her to establish a close contact with you which will stand you in good stead in the future if difficulties do arise.

There is evidence* that some of the most successful foster parents are those who have brought up their own families yet still have plenty of energy to spare. The reasons for this seem obvious enough; it is not just a question of experience in handling children. Such people may have gained confidence over the years in their capacity as parents and with the security of their own

* E.g. see Gordon Trasler, *In Place of Parents*, Routledge & Kegan Paul, 1960.

children's love and success behind them, can cope more easily with the insecurities of fostering. However, this does not mean that other people may not succeed equally well, for children have special and different needs which different foster parents can meet. For example, there are foster mothers of all ages, single or married or widowed who are particularly good at caring for small babies for short periods of time and enjoy it greatly.

If you have had unhappy times in your own childhood, especially if you have lived away from home, it is wise to be quite frank about this to the social worker. You may be able, just because of these experiences, to understand a child's feelings very deeply and sensitively and to help him greatly; on the other hand, it could be that fostering would reawaken unhappy feelings in you and would prove more than you could bear. If possible you should try to have an open discussion about this and to sort things out in your own mind. This may help you, as well as the children who need care.

The child and the foster family

If you have ever looked into a kaleidoscope, you will remember the way in which when you shook it, the pattern changed. That is what happens to a family when it takes a foster child. Every family works out a kind of balance between its members and any new person coming into it affects the way everybody feels towards each other. You may already have noticed this when you had your own children, especially perhaps the first baby which alters the way of life of a man and a woman so greatly. Or you may have noticed it if you had your

* These comments are especially relevant when the foster child is handicapped.

H

elderly parents to live with you.

One of the most important things about this family balance is to do with the dependence or independence of the members and with the giving and taking that goes on. Clearly, the younger the child, the more you expect him to be dependent and to 'take' rather than to 'give'. Yet it is not simply a matter of age — it is far more subtle than that. Individuals at any age vary a great deal in these respects. Some, for example, like to be fussed over when they are ill — like to be a bit dependent; others hate it. Some like best to give presents — others to receive. Families find out about each other and make adjustments. So it may happen that a man who works very hard and has a position of responsibility shows at home to his wife and family his need for cosseting and attention. Or it may be that an older child in the family for some reason is much more demanding than his younger brothers and sisters and everybody has come somehow to accept this and make allowances. These kinds of things are going on in families all the time and is one reason why the family is such an important source of strength to its members.

When a foster child comes into the home, who needs a great deal of attention, everybody is affected. Real, deep love is like the widow's cruse of oil — it never runs out; it can be shared and divided yet there is still plenty for everybody. But it takes time for a family to establish a new pattern of giving and taking. This may show itself over quite trivial matters; that the youngest child always had half an hour on his mother's knee alone after dinner and now he has to share it; that the seven-year-old always has the toy from the cereal packet and now the foster child is clamouring for it; that the fourteen-year-old plays pop records in the evening and now has to do it more quietly while the foster child gets off to sleep; that the husband has disturbed nights because the foster child is ill; or even that Granny who has in some ways been 'the baby' for a few years does not like having her position usurped.

Added to this, we know that the small newcomer will in all probability not be a model guest, for all the reasons which I discussed in chapter 3. He will react in particular ways to members of your family. Jealousy of someone near his own age or younger is to be expected. (This is partly why social workers are sometimes uneasy about placing foster children too near the age of the natural children.) But there may be other more subtle things going on. In chapter 3, I described how Linda began by seeming to prefer her foster father, then 'went off' him completely while she was ill, then returned to a more natural balance of affection between the two foster parents. She was an attractive, winning little girl and it would not have been surprising if her foster father felt first flattered and then a bit hurt at her changing reactions; or if her foster mother had felt put out at Linda's apparent indifference to her at first. Children call out strong feelings in those who care for them; they transfer to the foster parents the feelings they had about their own parents and work out some of their confusion and anger on the foster parents. This can be upsetting for foster parents and is a very different kind of experience from that of bringing up your own children. Families tend to take themselves for granted until someone joins them whose ways are different. The contrast then throws their habits and attitudes into relief. There are many different factors in these differences; some of which I discussed in chapter 4; these are related partly to the social class and education of the parents, partly to race and religion, and so on. But even apart from this, families, just like individuals, develop characteristic ways of behaving and acting, which are peculiar to them. This of course is due in part to the personalities of the parents but it is a complicated affair in which the developing children also play their part. For example, there are families which tend to be very 'outgoing', rather noisy, with lots of friends in and out; others may be quite the reverse. Or there are common family attitudes—for example to physical pain. Some people expect a child to cry easily when he is hurt and will readily pick him up to comfort him. Others feel that this encourages fusses about nothing and from quite an early age discourage tears and cuddles. (You would expect them to have 'a stiff upper lip' themselves in similar situations.) Some families will have different expectations from the children in this matter of bearing pain according to whether it is a boy or a girl, from quite an early age.

Physical pain is only one example of many; your family may, despite the individual differences of its members, have a set of attitudes in common vastly different from those your small foster child has been used to. So everyone must be prepared for surprises.

No one can tell beforehand what these surprises will be or how the family will be affected by them. The vital thing from your family's point of view is to remember that it is natural and inevitable that there will be mixed feelings from time to time about this small stranger in your midst. This has to be stressed because foster parents who offer a home to a child with warm, kindly feelings about his plight sometimes feel ashamed when they discover just how much he can upset them—perhaps his naughtiness makes them angry, perhaps his grieving is more than they can bear, perhaps his coldness hurts them. We all have to learn the hard lesson — of coping with mixed feelings about those we love. But it is particularly difficult sometimes for foster families for two reasons. First, because there often is not time for love to establish itself before it is put to the test by the child. Second, foster parents feel more guilty because of the pity and compassion they have for the child. They know 'it's not his fault' and are nevertheless astounded to find just how much a little child can upset them.

Sometimes you will be unfortunate in having a foster child who is particularly disturbed and makes great demands on the family's time and patience. (Christopher in chapter 3 is an example.) Sometimes the difficulty will be one of adjustment between you and the child. Take, for example, the question of intelligence.

> Mr and Mrs Jones had placed with them a little girl who was of limited intelligence. They had two small boys who were exceptionally clever. The foster mother to her horror heard one of the boys introducing her to his friend: 'This is Beryl — she's stupid.' At first she was very angry but then realised this was not nastiness but a statement of fact. Her son was trying to get over to his playmates that they could not expect the same of Beryl. This was his way of trying to adjust to the situation.

Sometimes the difficulty may be within the foster parents themselves, for we all have particular sore points, things that worry us specially in others' behaviour. Thus one foster mother does not mind a bit about wet or dirty pants but is very worried if the child does not finish his dinner; a foster father may be quite unworried by a naughty, disobedient little tough but finds a persistently crying baby hard to bear. Some find an unresponsive child difficult; others dislike a child who 'hangs round their neck all day'. Why are there these differences? The explanation often lies deep in our personality and in our own childhood experiences; we may or may not be able to see the connections for ourselves. But it has to be understood that what goes on between you and the child is an interaction. He feels things about you and you feel things about him. Some of what you feel is to do with the present situation — that he has wet his pants for the sixth time that day and it is a bad day for drying clothes, for instance — but some of it is to do with your feelings about your own parents and your childhood. This may sound strange yet, as with the chidren's parents, so foster parents' attitudes are much affected by their own experiences of being 'mothered' and 'fathered'.

It may be hard to admit these feelings to anyone and especially to the social worker, who may have placed the child with you. You may think that she is wanting everything to be all right and does not want to hear your troubles. In the long run, it will probably help you to tell someone about the reactions your family is having to the child and the social worker may be the best person to hear about it. But whether you tell someone or keep it to yourself, you should remember that it is normal to have these mixed feelings of love and anger, sympathy and impatience, enjoyment and anxiety and so on. You should not be frightened of them — but should admit them and recognise their existence in the other members of your family. Clare Winnicott once said: 'We are not looking for perfect parents, because they exist only in theory.'* It is not necessary to be 'perfect parents' to the foster child, just ordinary, and being ordinary includes being fed up with him as well as loving him.

* 'Casework in the Child Care Service', reprinted in *Child Care and Social Work*, Codicote Press, 1964.

Much of what I have been saying about mixed feelings applies to caring for any child — your own or someone else's. There is, however, a special anxiety in looking after someone else's which all good foster parents have. There is a deep sense of responsibility about taking on this task and a certain self-consciousness which comes from knowing that people's eyes are on you — the children's department, the neighbours and so on. This is something that foster parents have to learn to live with. It is one of the nastier sides of human nature that people who do not take foster children are sometimes particularly quick to criticise those who do. They claim genuine concern for the welfare of the child but sometimes there are other less wholesome motives, like jealousy or envy of those who do the work. It is as well for foster parents to be prepared for this; you may be lucky in your area — it may never happen to you — but if it does, it may help you to know that yours is not a unique case — there are always people ready to criticise.

Relationships with the parents

In the last chapter I discussed three of the four things which makes it difficult for foster parents to understand the parents' point of view. The fourth concerned your feelings about the parents: for this can affect the way you see them. Experience has shown us that in most cases foster parents feel differently about parents after they have actually met them. Sometimes, quite frightening pictures have been built up in the foster parents' minds and the reality comes as quite a relief. For example, a father who has been violent to a child proves to be a pathetic ineffectual man whose outburst was an isolated one, due to particular stress; or a woman who has lived an immoral life proves to be not 'a brazen huzzy' but an unintelligent bedraggled tragic person. This kind of thing has happened so often that we have come to believe wherever possible parents and foster parents should meet. There will of course be occasions when this is undesirable and times when the reality is as bad as the imaginary picture but that is not generally the case.

Nevertheless, there remains the inescapable fact that even when parents are life-size figures, not ogres, there are ingredients in the situation which are explosive. For there is nothing which calls out more primitive feelings in all of us than the care of children. It is quite inevitable. How you feel will of course depend on the kind of fostering you are doing and your reasons for doing it, but there are three main causes of difficulty within yourselves—sometimes more than one at a time.

(1) You really want to make the child your own and dislike sharing him with his parents.

(2) You find the distress the parents cause the child hard to bear.

(3) You find the parents' attitude to you hard to bear.

If you are childless or not good at sharing, you may do best to think of adoption not fostering; that is obvious from what I have said earlier. But it is not as simple as that. Sometimes you may take a child knowing full well he will return to his parents, and with the security of your own family and children behind him, and still find that in some way this particular child has found a special place in your affection and that you will be desolate when he goes. This happens when a child stays much longer than was originally planned; or occasionally foster mothers who have taken dozens of short-stay children and been fond of them all find that one has moved them deeply for no reason they can understand. There is really nothing to be done about this for it is in the nature of the task. The most helpful thing in the long run is to admit to yourself that you are hurt and sore inside at the thought of losing him and not to pretend it's 'only the child you are thinking of'. This is a risk which all foster parents take; but many feel it is a risk well worth taking because of the satisfactions they get from the work.

The problems of the parents which I have described make it inevitable that in different ways some of them will cause their children suffering and distress. It may not be deliberate, but as a result of their illness or inadequacy. That does not make it any the less painful to the children. There will be occasions when it is decided that the parents cannot be allowed to see their children because of this. But most times, foster parents will be asked to keep in touch with parents and to cope with the effect this contact has on the child because in the long run it will be for the best. The experienced foster parent learns to protect the child in all kinds of ways; for example, when a parent is unreliable about visiting, the foster parent says nothing about it beforehand to avoid disappointment. Yet there are limits to the amount of protecting that can be done; with some parents there will be promises broken, unsuitable behaviour and so on, whatever the good foster parent does. The foster parents' ability to stand by the child and help him through these episodes is crucial. You are not expected to be plaster saints and there will be times when you will be furious on the child's behalf. Yet in the long run you will help him most not by standing up for him against his parents but by helping him show his feelings openly about them when he needs to and by sharing his suffering with him. For the very young child this may just mean holding him and letting him cry rather than any direct words spoken. But by the

time he is four or five years old, more direct
communication is possible. For example, when his Daddy
did not visit as he had promised, you may be able to help
him say he is cross with Daddy or worried about Daddy or
whatever he is feeling. But you will be able to do this
effectively only if you can concentrate on how he is feeling
and are not swamped by your own reactions.

I have already suggested that foster parents are
naturally anxious about the care they give another's child
and may be particularly sensitive to criticism. If you
recognise this it will help you to cope with criticisms
which may seem to you unjust as you will be freer to look
at the parents' fears and resentment which caused them
to find fault.

None of these difficulties are inevitable; quite often,
especially in 'short-stay', foster parents and parents
manage their relationships quite easily and may even
keep in touch with each other afterwards as friends. But
there is no need to write of the many instances where
there are no problems, for in such cases the ordinary
common sense and goodwill of both parties is enough. My
concern has been to look at everyone involved in the
situation and see how each may affect the other, and
what tensions may arise and why.

Foster parents and the law
Since this book was first written, there has been
increasing emphasis on the rights of the child to greater
legal protection from impulsive or disruptive action by his
parents. This has culminated in the passing of the
Children Act 1975, which has had a good deal of
publicity in the media.

It seems important, at the end of a short book, to

re-state briefly some essentials in the legal relationships between children, their parents and foster parents and to mention the most important changes in the law which concern foster parents.

The first point which has to be made is that a child is legally bound to his parents, until an adoption order is made. Only that order finally ends the parents' rights and their responsibilities. The new law does help to protect foster parents and children, in ways which I shall describe later. But fostering is, *by definition*, taking care of someone else's child. That fact must be faced from the beginning.

In chapter 1, I described the kinds of children who come into care of local authorities. From a legal point of view, there are really three important groups. First (the majority), there are children who come into care voluntarily at the request of their parents. They must go home if their parents request it. (Sickness of parents is the commonest cause.) They usually go home quickly. Second, in respect of those children who come into care at their parents' request, the local authority takes over parental rights of a number when the parents are, for various reasons, considered unfit to resume care of them. Third, there are children who come into care by order of a court when they are considered to be in need of care or control. So far as young children are concerned, this means children who have been in some way neglected or ill-treated. Parental rights for such children are in the hands of the local authority until such time as the court revokes the order. (Before the court decides to make a long-term order, foster parents may sometimes be asked to care for a child on a short-term order.)

A child you foster may fall into any one of these three groups. The changes in the law are mainly concerned with the first two. Put simply they are as follows — but do remember the law is never simple; you should always seek advice from social workers or solicitors about specific cases.*

(1) If you have had a foster child for more than six months, even under voluntary agreement by the parents with the local authority, parents must now give twenty-eight days notice before they remove him. This can only be good for all concerned and should prevent impulsive acts by parents, which are not in the child's interests, and anxiety and stress for the foster parents.

(2) The local authority can now take over parental rights if a child has been in care 'voluntarily' for more than three years, even if there is no definite evidence that the parents' state of health or way of life makes them unfit to have him — which used to be the case. To quote from a government circular: † 'it is envisaged that this power will be used only where the parents have not been undertaking parental care and have shown little interest in the child's welfare throughout the three years and it has become necessary . . . to reach decisions about the child's long term future. . . .'

This is a real protection for child and foster parents. But it needs to be thought about very carefully for we cannot assume that all parents who fail in regular contact with a child for three years are going to be unsuitable for ever to have their children back, or that the children might not want to return. However, this book is about young children and it seems highly likely that if a child has lived happily with foster parents for three years of a short life, he will feel he 'belongs' to them. Bear in mind, though, that the three-year period is in the care of the

* For example, if you foster privately, the position will be quite different.

† DHSS local authority circular (75)21.

local authority, not necessarily in one foster home. Sadly, he might have been bounced around from pillar to post in care and, in such cases, if his mother (for example) settled down, that might be best for him. In short, this is a legal provision which is fraught with practical and emotional difficulties. We shall have to see how it works out. Foster parents bear a heavy moral burden not to discourage parents from visiting so that they can claim 'little contact'.

(3) If you have looked after a child for three years or more you can apply to the court for custody. If the court agrees, the child may not be removed from your home unless you agree. Similarly, if you have had the child for at least five years, you can apply to the court for permission to adopt and, until the matter is decided, the child cannot be removed. Of course, if an order is granted, the child becomes as your natural child.

This new position clearly protects foster parents from the sudden removal of a child whom they wish to make their own and removes the 'baby-snatching' element in the 'tug of love'. One must remember, however, that no law changes the emotional aspects of the 'tug of love'. But, again, so far as young children are concerned, it is obviously right that they should not be subjected to sudden change, whilst such decisions are being made. One again, such situations are likely to be complicated and legal advice may be important.

So much for the points in the new law which most affect you. There is much that is unchanged which you should know too: for example, parents have a legal responsibility to notify the local authority of their address. The other side of the coin is that, as a foster parent, you have responsibilities as well as rights and these will be explained to you when you apply. For example, the child must be visited by a social worker and examined by a doctor at regular intervals. The ideal is a partnership between foster parents and the local authority. But because children must be protected, the social services department does have real *authority* (for example, to remove a child if they do not think he is cared for properly, or if he is not settling down happily, or if it would be best for him to join a brother, or sister, or relative).

However, recent changes have given foster parents some alternative channel of protest — to the courts, if they, on occasions, do not feel they are getting a fair deal from the local authorities and, if such situations arise, they should certainly consult a solicitor. It is also useful to note that there is now a National Foster Care Association,* which is well placed to advise on such matters, as well as an Association of British Adoption and Fostering Agencies.†

Once a foster parent becomes a prospective adopter, there are many other legal matters to be considered. But that is outside the scope of this book.

Why foster?
If this task of fostering is so beset with difficulties and problems of one kind or another, why do it? Should the motive be one of pure unselfishness, a desire to help a child, no matter what the cost? I do not believe that there is such a thing as 'unselfishness', for, from any kind of activity, we should expect satisfaction and rewards of some kind. What can be expected from fostering?

(1) Your family may benefit: families do make the

* 129 Queen's Crescent, London NW5.

† 4 Southampton Row, London WC1B 4AA.

adjustments necessary to fit a foster child into their family and gain greatly from it. Someone else's need for love and attention often brings out a generosity which was lying dormant and the whole family can be united in their desire to find the newcomer a place in their midst. The experience of fostering may enrich and deepen family affection through the sense of a common purpose and the knowledge that they have overcome together their initial difficulties.

(2) In one way or another, we all have a need to feel we are valuable people, doing valuable work. Fostering is one way of satisfying this need and it is a particularly useful way for women who feel that they are 'home-centred' and that their talents show up most clearly in that setting.

(3) Fostering is extremely interesting and stimulating. The role of the foster parent is changing rapidly and, as this book has implied throughout, it is more than kind parenthood. It offers a challenge to people who feel the need of new horizons, while remaining within the circle of their homes. It brings you in contact with children, their relations and social workers, whom you would otherwise never have met. It requires you to think about children and adults, including yourself, in new ways.

(4) For some, of whom I am one, the fascination of the young child under five is unending. His development is so rapid by comparison with other ages, his sense of wonder and excitement so infectious, his feelings so open and candid that to care for him may be particularly satisfying. To know that you have played a part in freeing him from the anxiety or fear or grief or bewilderment which have hindered his development can be profoundly rewarding.

He is someone else's child and nothing can alter that

but you and he may create together something unique that will stand him in good stead for the rest of his life. Your care may have helped him to cope with separation and to return undamaged to his loving parents. Or it may be that you have given him some sense of security and trust in the adult world which will keep him afloat in a sea of troubles when he returns home. Or it may be that you will be able to offer him a permanent home in which he can develop his full potentialities. Of one thing we can now, with our present knowledge, be sure: even if he appears to forget you in the top of his mind, he will never forget you within the deeper parts of his mind, where childhood memories are hidden yet continue to influence our lives. You are there, alive in him, for ever. This is your responsibility and your reward.

Note
There is a dearth of books written specifically for foster parents but a number of publications are coming from the Association of British Adoption and Fostering Agencies and from the National Foster Care Association (see p. 120, footnote).